COLIN ARMSTRONG is a lifelong Rangers supporter and a former columnist for both the *Rangers News* and the Rangers match-day programme. He contributed to the book *Ten Days That Shook Rangers* (Fort, 2005) and has written extensively on the subject of Rangers for other publications including *When Saturday Comes* and *The Rangers Standard*. Born in Glasgow, he now lives in Falkirk with his wife, Shona, and their children, Connor and Sophie.

IAIN DUFF is an award-winning journalist with almost twenty years of experience writing for publications in both England and Scotland. He joined Glasgow's *Evening Times* as a news reporter in 1995 and two years later became the paper's chief reporter at the age of 25. The same year he won the prestigious UK Press Gazette Scoop of the Year award and was nominated as Scotland's young journalist of the year. He later joined the Press Association where he was Scottish editor for six years. His books include *Follow on: Fifty Years of Rangers in Europe* (Fort, 2006) and *Temple of Dreams: The Changing Face of Ibrox* (DB Publishing, 2008).

DAVID EDGAR was the spokesman for the Rangers Supporters Trust from 2005 to 2010, during which time he campaigned on a number of issues regarding the stewardship of the club under Sir David Murray. He played an active role in speaking out against what many Rangers fans saw as unflattering coverage in the mainstream media. His book on Rangers over the last 30 years *21st Century Blue: Being a Bear in the Modern World* (DB Publishing, 2010) is a funny and often controversial look at the club throughout an unforgettable era. He is currently the host of *Heart and Hand – the Rangers Podcast*, a light-hearted weekly look at Scottish Football.

W STEWART FRANKLIN is co-founder of *The Rangers Standard*, a former Rangers Supporters Trust board member and co-owner of Gersnet.co.uk. He has been taking an active part in the Rangers supporting community for several years. In addition to administrating his own site, Stewart has written articles for STV Sport and *The Herald* as well as appearing on TV and radio. A Rangers season ticket holder of 15 years, he can be found bouncing away beside the rest of the Blue Order 'every other Saturday'.

JOHN DC GOW is a freelance writer who is a co-founder of *The Rangers Standard* and a regular contributor to ESPN on Scottish football and Rangers FC. He has contributed to football magazines such as the *Away End* and non-football current affairs magazine *Scottish Review*. He is particularly interested in studying sectarianism, both in ending the backward form of hatred and in how it relates to freedom of speech, censorship and Rangers.

CHRIS GRAHAM is a co-founder of *The Rangers Standard* and writer for *Seventy2* magazine and *The Copland Road Organization* (CRO). He has made numerous appearances on *Scotland Tonight* and has also appeared on *Newsnight Scotland*, *Reporting Scotland*, STV News and *The Rising* (a Rangers TV documentary) to discuss a variety of Rangers-related issues. He has appeared on BBC Radio, written about Rangers for the *Scotland on Sunday* and made guest appearances on Rangers podcasts. A season ticket holder at Ibrox, he was part of the Rangers Supporters Trust campaign to encourage fan participation in the Rangers share issue.

ROSS EJ HENDRY is a lifelong supporter of Rangers FC. He lives in Toronto, Canada and is a member of the Toronto Central Rangers Supporters Club. He is a standing member of the *We Are The People* Podcast which was established in 2008 and was the first podcast fully dedicated to the trials and triumphs of Rangers FC. He is currently a director with a global company specialising in brand and commercial development, route to market optimisation and installation of brand/market combinations.

DAVID KINNON is a Scottish Chartered Accountant, licensed insolvency practitioner and Johnstone Smith Professor of Accountancy within the University of Glasgow Business School. His professional experience covers board-level positions within listed and private-equity backed companies. For over 20 years he has advised on business reorganisation and financial restructuring matters, working internationally, based in London. Of the many great Rangers players seen over years of supporting the Club, including as a debenture holder from the Club Deck, Richard Gough and Brian Laudrup are his all-time favourites.

ALASDAIR MCKILLOP is a co-founder of *The Rangers Standard* and writer for *Seventy2* magazine. He is a regular contributor to the online current affairs magazine *Scottish Review* where he writes about sport and politics. He is a contributor to *Bigotry, Football and Scotland* (Edinburgh University Press, 2013).

GAIL RICHARDSON is a popular blogger and prominent member of the online Rangers community. She is a member of the Rangers Supporters Trust which promotes fan ownership. A lifelong Rangers fan, she attended her first game at Ibrox when she was six years old.

CALVIN SPENCE was previously the Deputy Northern Ireland Secretary of the British Medical Association. His expertise lies in the field of Employment Law, Industrial Relations and Human Resources, and although retired, he continues to provide management consultancy services to General Practitioners and Hospital Trusts within the Northern Ireland Health & Social Care system. A Rangers fan for over 38 years, he continues to travel from Belfast to watch the team. He is a regular contributor to *Rangers Media* and *The Rangers Standard*.

RICHARD WILSON was born in Glasgow and spent almost 10 years at *The Sunday Times Scotland*, as deputy sports editor, then staff sports writer. In 2002, he won the Jim Rodger Memorial Award for best young sports writer. In 2003, at the Scottish Press Awards, he was named Sports Writer of the Year and he has regularly been nominated in the Sports Feature Writer of the Year category. He now writes extensively about football, and occasionally boxing and golf, for *The Herald* and *Sunday Herald* and is the author of *Inside the Divide: One City, Two Teams... The Old Firm* (Canongate, 2012).

Follow We Will

The Fall and Rise of Rangers

Edited by

W STEWART FRANKLIN, JOHN DC GOW
CHRIS GRAHAM and ALASDAIR McKILLOP

Luath Press Limited
EDINBURGH
www.luath.co.uk

First published 2013

ISBN: 978-1-908373-68-7

The paper used in this book is recyclable. It is made from
low chlorine pulps produced in a low energy, low emissions manner
from renewable forests.

Printed and bound by
Martins the Printers, Berwick upon Tweed

Typeset in 11 point Sabon
by 3btype.com

The authors' right to be identified as author of this book under the
Copyright, Designs and Patents Act 1988 has been asserted.

To Beverley, Amira and Ziara – courage, inspiration and love provided for on a daily basis. Also for my parents, William and Sheena – I could not have asked for better guidance.

Finally in remembrance of my brother Ian – hugely missed but never forgotten.

Stewart Franklin

I dedicate this book to Jessica and Harry who I love very much.

Also love and thanks to my parents, Maureen and Hendry, my sister Mary, big Iain and wee Iain, Murdy, Christine, Robert, Lisa, Frances and my Gran.

John DC Gow

To Siobhan and Archie for their love and patience. Also to my parents for a lifetime of good advice, love and support.

Chris Graham

To Natalie and my parents Carol and Graham for everything and with love always.

And to my granda Dan McKillop – truly one of the Clyde's finest.

Alasdair McKillop

Contents

Acknowledgements

As editors, our burden has been lessened considerably by the excellent work and good humour of the people who contributed chapters to this book. We asked a lot of them but, like any great team, they rose to the occasion. To all of them we offer our sincere thanks. We feel it is appropriate to take this opportunity to thank all those who have taken the time to contribute to *The Rangers Standard* since it was launched in June 2012. If the site has a good name then it's because of the quality of the work produced by the Rangers community in general. We are simply in the fortunate position of being able to publish some of it. A special mention goes to those non-Rangers fans who have offered a different take on developments, particularly Dr Andrew Sanders and Harry Reid who have taken the plunge on more than one occasion. When dealing with Scottish football, it is useful to be reminded that friendly disagreement is still possible. In addition, Harry played a vital role in the early stages of this project and it might not have become what it is without his intervention.

Our good friend Graham Campbell acted as an unofficial editor by offering helpful comments and constructive criticism on more than one draft of this book. This assistance has to be added to all the wise advice and encouragement he has supplied over the past year. Working with two other good friends has been both an honour and, at times, an educational experience. In many ways, we follow in their footsteps. Our thanks to them are no less genuine because they aren't named here; we're confident they will know who they are.

Gordon Irvine has frequently been a source of both inspiration and incredible information over the past year. He has gone down some very interesting rabbit holes on behalf of the Rangers support. Dialogue with Scott Reid played an important part in shaping the arguments put forward in one chapter which he subsequently commented on. Cameron Stewart and Kenny Robertson cast a critical eye over the book and probably saved us from a bit of trouble. Amanda Ferguson kindly spoke to a few people on our behalf in the early stages and Andy McGowan gets a mention here despite earning it by dubious means.

Shane Nicholson and Peter Ewart from *The Copland Road Organization,* James Donaldson from *Seventy2* magazine, Stuart MacLean of Red and Black Rangers, Peter Smith of STV and Robert Boyle, the club's Social Media Officer, all gave us their time and thoughts and the book is considerably better as a result. Bill Murray, a man who did so much to encourage serious writing about Rangers and Celtic, read and commented on one of the chapters from his base on the other side of the world. His vast experience observing Glasgow's Giants and his distance from the current bitterness of Scottish football mean he still has an invaluable sense of perspective.

Lee Wallace, in addition to being an outstanding player who was loyal to the club at its lowest ebb, sat down for an interview despite being under no obligation to do so. He also provided one of the iconic moments in the dark months after administration by celebrating his goal against Celtic with a passion that was football at its very best. Legend status is fast approaching. Rangers' Press Officer Carol Patton did her utmost to facilitate a meeting with a member of the playing squad and was a generous host at Murray Park. Also at the club, James Traynor helped in a number of ways despite a heavy workload and Stephen Kerr helped to arrange a launch none of us were expecting. We are grateful to both for their assistance. We were delighted when Connal Cochrane, the manager of the Rangers Charity Foundation, agreed to accept the authors' proceeds stemming from this book to support the charity's valuable work.

Willie Vass let us use two of the many photographs from his wonderful collection at a friendly price. All Rangers fans should take the time to wander through his meticulously organised archives which are readily available online. They will become a priceless asset for future generations trying to get a sense of what it was like following Rangers on this remarkable journey.

Gavin MacDougall, Kirsten Graham and Louise Hutcheson were our stalwarts at Luath Press. Four novices require more time and attention than one but they were more than up to the challenge. The finished product is testimony to their skill and professionalism. Thanks too for all the coffee and for letting us share your view from Castlehill.

Foreword by Walter Smith

THE RANGERS STORY is one that continues to attract interest from more than just the club's fans. This is a tale which fascinates so many no matter which clubs they support, or even which sports they prefer, and this level of interest is further proof of just how massive Rangers really are and not just in Scotland.

Television crews and journalists from all around the globe have been dispatched to Ibrox and Murray Park to report on the club which refused to be killed off.

And these journalists have been amazed by what they have found. They have marvelled at the unbreakable spirit and passion of a vast army of supporters as well as the commitment and belief of the Rangers staff. They have all endured and they will, I am certain, see their club return to the pinnacle of Scottish football.

But of course the club continues to be beset by controversy and there are times, probably because of the catastrophic consequences caused by the actions of a few, when you feel as though it has always been this way. It's as though we have been under siege and constantly fighting and struggling just to stay alive.

However, when you stand back, take a moment and draw breath, reality returns and it is possible to see this club for what it is. It is massive. It's proud. And it is still here, far from down and out.

This club has shown it's true strengths in the last few years when many others would have buckled and folded. We didn't because we know what we are and who we are. We are Rangers and we will prevail because of our spirit and belief.

We can talk about our failings, as you will find in this book written by people who care deeply about Rangers but who also believe questions must be asked. This a book about Rangers and the troubles we are enduring but it is a book which also highlights how important and powerful this club remains.

Significantly, attitudes towards Rangers are examined within these pages and while you will not agree with each author's views on certain issues or individuals it is thought provoking. There are parts I would dispute and comments on one or two individuals with which I might take issue but then this continually evolving Rangers story divides opinion.

But the truth of what happened should not be split or diced into parts so small that we can no longer see what actually happened.

With that in mind a group of people, Rangers fans, have taken it upon themselves to detail what occurred and ask questions. It is a worthy and valid exercise as we continue our journey back to full rehabilitation and if nothing else this read should warn us we must be more vigilant than ever before.

We know through first-hand experience that there are people out there, predators you might say of one or two, who saw Rangers as a way to make a quick gain. They are gone and Rangers are still here.

That we are is testament to the people who work at Ibrox and Murray Park but the fans can feel especially proud. Without them Rangers would have gone under and the manner in which they rallied should never be forgotten or dismissed. Our supporters have been and continue to be in a league of their own and I am immensely proud of what they have achieved.

There are still many obstacles to be overcome but Rangers, I am certain, will continue their upward path although progress will be smoother and quicker as soon as off-field distractions are dealt with properly. Again, I'm sure these problems will be solved and Rangers will return to the top healthier and probably also the most transparent club in the country.

As Rangers fans that's what we all wish and hope for and it would be good if anyone who wants to invest in or back this club in any way could bear this in mind. Rangers and their fans have suffered enough but all that has gone before has made us stronger and more determined to ensure the safety and future of this club. Questions will be asked and suspicions aroused no matter who steps forward and that can't be a bad thing.

Some financial institution, some individual might hold more shares than anyone else but no matter who owns what or how much in terms of shares, this club belongs to the supporters. This club isn't for the pleasure of a few, it is for the masses and that should not be forgotten.

It might be a long time before Rangers fans trust fully in anyone claiming to have the club's best interests at heart and that is understandable. It is for the directors and investors to prove they are worthy of backing because the fans don't have to prove anything to anyone. They have shown their loyalty and love for Rangers and they are the ones who keep the club alive no matter who comes to or goes from the boardroom.

This club has been scrutinised at various levels over the last few years in particular and no doubt Rangers will continue to be examined in the years ahead, which will be no bad thing. But let's please have intelligent debate rather than the ill-informed nonsense that's been filling newspapers, websites and airwaves.

Reasoned debate about our club has been substituted by gossip, which in the minds of too many quickly becomes fact, but at least this book attempts to bring balance and objectivity back into play. The major issues and controversies are covered within these pages by people who share a common agenda: They simply want to record what has happened in recent times in a clear and coherent fashion.

They deal with EBT, CVA, SFL, FTTT, SFA, RFFF, SPL and other acronyms which have become part of the language when talking about Rangers but this is very much a calm, composed narrative which goes a long way to explaining much of what has gone on around the club over these last few years. A lot of what has been written in the MSM (mainstream media, I believe) has been outlandish and inaccurate but this book is more than that.

Read it and see for yourselves.

Walter Smith
Rangers Chairman

Foreword by Graham Walker

IN THE AFTERMATH of Rangers going into administration, a traumatised support struggled to come to terms with the crisis. Confusion abounded. There was widespread disbelief that matters could have reached such a point. Emotions swung from despair to defiant optimism and back again as putative saviours emerged only to retreat to the shadows. Perhaps unsurprisingly given the huge size of Rangers' fan base, there was a variety of groups expressing different views on what had befallen the club and different prescriptions about how it might recover. However, clear-sighted analysis was in short supply.

It was therefore salutary that there should appear a new fans' website, called *The Rangers Standard*, committed to helping the club back to its feet but in a spirit of critical inquiry and unsparing self-examination. The site brought together a group of dedicated and highly knowledgeable supporters whose reflections and perspectives are featured in this volume along with those of others with similar expertise and communication skills. All of them are owed a vote of thanks by the Rangers support as a whole for their robust advocacy and passionate rejoinders to those who have rejoiced in the club's trials.

The *Standard* quickly became one of the most authoritative forums for Rangers fans after it launched in 2012. It provided a channel for fans to respond to events in a controlled, measured and insightful manner at a time when anger, disillusionment, fear and downright panic were never far away. On top of the acute feelings of betrayal felt by fans towards those who had run their club into the ground was piled the ordeal of enduring the spiteful response of so many connected with the Scottish game and beyond in wider society. In some ways the latter ordeal was the worst: few fans quite expected the volume of hostility that materialised, and many friendships were sorely tested, and in some cases severed. Knee jerk gloating over a rival's troubles is to be expected; the reaction to Rangers' plight was on an altogether deeper level of antagonism. It signalled a broad-based willingness to scapegoat Rangers for the ills of the Scottish game, and reflected the extent to which many had bought into the characterisation of the club as an institution largely responsible for the religious intolerance in Scottish society. Blaming Rangers was a facile and convenient way for many people to avoid facing the deep-seated problems of Scottish football, and to account for the phenomenon of sectarianism that was concurrently a political and media fetish. Many no doubt convinced themselves, if the posts on websites and blogs are any guide, that the demise of Rangers would actually be for the good of Scottish football, and would rid Scotland of its supposed sectarianism 'shame'. Contributors to the *Standard* site, which insisted on lengthy, properly argued pieces, took to task such shallow and bigoted assertions, and the chapter in this book by John DC Gow deserves to be read by anyone interested in dispassionately examining and exploring the sectarianism question in relation to Rangers and to Scottish society as opposed to using it to bolster tribal prejudice.

However, the *Standard* has not merely been a vehicle for contributors to defend the club. It is also a site that has encouraged fans to consider the changes that need to occur if Rangers are to recover their position as the premier sporting institution in Scotland. Such changes do not just refer to the enormous challenges on the field of play; they also involve re-assessment of the club's role in society, its values, what it ought to stand for, its identity. Here the *Standard* has sought contributions from people with no allegiance to Rangers and in some cases a plain dislike of the club. However, as long as the contributors in question presented well-reasoned arguments and did not resort to the gratuitous abuse so prevalent elsewhere, such pieces were viewed as important challenges to the beliefs and assumptions of Rangers fans regarding their club and its image, and timely nudges towards self-criticism and greater awareness of why resentments had built up.

Thus distinguished commentators and academics like Harry Reid and Alan Bairner raised pertinent points about Rangers' Protestant identity. Was the unsympathetic reaction of fans of non Old Firm teams, asked Bairner, a sign that such fans had resented what they saw as the hijacking of the Scottish Presbyterian tradition for the cause of Ulster Loyalism? No Rangers fan who cares about his or her club should dismiss such a question. Similarly, why have some Rangers fans, in their legitimate desire to defend their British allegiances, sought at the same time to disparage the Scottish national content of that compound identity? It is through the *Standard* and other blogs and through reading much-needed books such as this one, that fans might attempt to grapple with questions that pose dilemmas and maybe require hard choices.

At the time of writing Rangers' troubles persist. Again fans are unable to get straight answers to questions about ownership, investment, and future direction. Just as it is the club's supporters who have been hurt most of all by what has happened and just as it is those supporters who have ensured its survival by their magnificent show of loyalty, perhaps only when the fans whose voices can be heard so compellingly in these pages hold a controlling stake will Rangers truly prosper. Only then might the club 'follow follow' the shining example set by its founders, the lads who had a dream and nothing to back it except determination and desire.

Graham Walker
Professor of Political History at Queen's University Belfast
and Co-author of *The Official Biography of Rangers*

Glossary

ADMINISTRATION:	An insolvency procedure under which court-appointed Administrators attempt to preserve the company as a going concern, or to get a better return for the creditors than by liquidation.
BDO:	The firm of which Malcolm Cohen and James Stephen, Joint Liquidators of RFC 2012 Limited (In Liquidation), formerly The Rangers Football Club PLC, are partners. As Joint Liquidators, they will collect in all monies and sell all remaining assets, and use proceeds to pay a dividend to creditors. They have wide-ranging powers to investigate the circumstances surrounding the financial collapse of the company.
BIG TAX CASE (BTC):	The popular name used when referring to the dispute with HM Revenue and Customs over the administration of Employee Benefit Trusts. This is a dispute between RFC 2012 and HMRC.
COMPANY VOLUNTARY ARRANGEMENT (CVA):	An agreement proposed by a company to its creditors under which creditors agree to accept a pence-in-the-pound payment in full and final settlement of the monies owed. The CVA proposed by the Joint Administrators with the financial support of Charles Green's consortium failed in June 2012 because HM Revenue and Customs voted against it.
DUFF & PHELPS:	The firm of which Paul Clark and David Whitehouse are partners; they were appointed Joint Administrators of The Rangers Football Club PLC in February 2012.
EMPLOYEE BENEFIT: TRUST (EBT)	A discretionary trust for the benefit of employees used by Oldco Rangers between 2002 and

2010. Their use was the subject of the First Tier Tax Tribunal proceedings and a Scottish Premier League Commission chaired by Lord Nimmo Smith.

FIRST TIER TAX TRIBUNAL (FTTT):
The body which heard Rangers' appeal against a tax bill from HM Revenue and Customs over the use of EBTs. The tribunal found in favour of Rangers in the vast majority of cases, determining EBT payments to be payments to beneficiaries other than the player. Payments to the player from the trust under the EBT arrangements were held to be loans as opposed to remuneration and therefore not liable for tax in the form of PAYE and NI. HM Revenue and Customs have appealed the verdict.

INSOLVENCY:
A company is insolvent when it cannot pay its debts as they fall due or where the company's assets are less than its liabilities, with no prospect of that being reversed.

LIQUIDATION:
The insolvency process under which a company ceases to trade, and under which Liquidators sell the assets of the company and distribute the proceeds to creditors.

OLDCO RANGERS:
RFC 2012 Limited (In Liquidation), formerly Rangers Football Club PLC: the company which owned and operated the Club until the company entered into Administration.

'NO TO NEWCO':
A movement comprising non-Rangers fans who opposed Rangers re-entry into the Scottish Premier League. It was mainly an online movement.

RANGERS:
The football club founded in 1872 now operated by Rangers International Football Club PLC.

RANGERS FANS FIGHTING FUND (RFFF):
Prominent fundraising body comprising fans and senior Rangers figures. It paid some small creditors and provided the funds for a QC and

solicitor to attend the SPL Commission chaired by Lord Nimmo Smith.

RANGERS SUPPORTERS TRUST (RST): One of the three main Rangers fans organisations. It exists to promote fan ownership and raised £250,000 during the Initial Public Offering of shares in December 2012 through the Buy Rangers campaign.

RED AND BLACK RANGERS: A fan-led campaign to raise money for Rangers by selling scarves and using the money to buy tickets for games at Ibrox.

SCOTTISH FOOTBALL ASSOCIATION (SFA): Scottish football's governing body which 'exists to promote, foster and develop the game at all levels'. Stewart Regan is the chief executive.

SCOTTISH FOOTBALL LEAGUE (SFL): The football body responsible for the operation of the First, Second and Third Divisions in Scottish football. David Longmuir is the chief executive. Rangers were admitted to the Third Division as an associate member following a 25–5 vote in July 2012.

SCOTTISH PREMIER LEAGUE (SPL): The top league in Scottish football from the 1998–9 season onwards. Neil Doncaster, the chief executive, was the key SPL figure throughout the Rangers crisis.

THE BLUE KNIGHTS: A consortium of Rangers-supporting business-men, fronted by former Rangers director Paul Murray, bidding for the assets of the company in administration. The group was widely considered the popular choice among Rangers fans.

TICKETUS: A London-based firm, part of Octopus Invest-ments, that bulk buys tickets in advance for events and collects the proceeds when the tickets are sold to the public. Craig Whyte sold three years' worth of Rangers season tickets as part of £26.7m deal to fund his takeover. At one stage, the firm was a member of The Blue

Knights consortium before the contract put in place by Whyte was terminated by the Joint Administrators after application to the Court and Ticketus became the second largest creditor of The Rangers Football Club PLC.

Introduction

WITH A 141-year history which has been characterised by the almost compulsive accumulation of silverware and accolades, Rangers are the world's most domestically successful football club. To date, they have won 54 Scottish League titles, 33 Scottish Cups and 27 Scottish League Cups, plus the European Cup Winners' Cup in 1972.

In previous eras, the club did much to spread the game through pioneering tours of North America, and Scotland once basked in the reflected glory of triumphs over the best England and the Soviet Union had to offer. From the late 1980s until 2011, one man dominated the club as majority shareholder and long periods as chairman: Sir David Murray. His arrival in 1988 has been well chronicled and the important part played by Graeme Souness is common knowledge. Working in conjunction with Souness and Walter Smith, Murray brought steel and ambition to Ibrox.

The club became an extension of the personality of the man who had excelled in the world of business, with everything that usually entails. He was competitive and eager for a place among the elite in any context. Murray oversaw a period of remarkable success, with Rangers matching Celtic's record of nine successive league championships between 1989 and 1997. Great players such as Richard Gough, Ally McCoist, Brian Laudrup and Paul Gascoigne evoked memories of previous eras of Rangers dominance and suggested a return to the natural order of things after a long period of underachievement.

The pursuit of European success became all-consuming once the thrill of dominating Scottish football diminished towards the end of the 1990s. Murray devoted unprecedented resources to the task and the highly regarded Dutch manager Dick Advocaat was employed to spend them. There is little doubt that the calibre of player was impressive and Ibrox regulars grew accustomed to watching teams illuminated by the likes of Arthur Numan, Ronald de Boer and the precociously talented Barry Ferguson. But European success remained stubbornly elusive despite a few captivating performances. There wasn't even a run comparable to that seen in 1992–3 when a predominantly Scottish side managed by Walter Smith made it to within one game of the inaugural Champions League final. The wilful abandonment of traditional Scottish frugalness was best symbolised by the £12m acquisition of Tore André Flo in November 2000. The Norwegian striker was by no means a bad player but the outlay underlined both a loss of perspective and financial gambling in the rundown casino that was Scottish football. Indeed it was during Advocaat's tenure as manager that Rangers began making payments to players though Employee Benefit Trusts (EBTS), at the time an entirely legal tax minimisation scheme introduced to the club by Murray International Holdings (MIH). The use of EBTS would continue until they were outlawed under new legislation passed in 2010 but they would go on to play a critical role in the public perception of Rangers' wrong-doing when the financial reckoning arrived in early 2012.

Such excess naturally resulted in a debilitating hangover and subsequent managers were forced to deal with the symptoms. Rangers were left financially vulnerable by the big spending of the Advocaat era. Managers such as Alex McLeish and Walter Smith, upon his return to the club in 2007, had to manage both a downsizing process and the expectations of a support that didn't always grasp the new reality. Sir David Murray quit as Rangers chairman in 2002 but continued as owner. He returned to his former role in 2004 after his company, MIH, was compelled to underwrite a £57m share issue with the club's debts standing at £74m. A third place finish in 2005–6, albeit a season that also saw Rangers become the first Scottish side to reach the last 16 of the Champions League, testified to the perilous position of the club as painfully as any balance sheet. Walter Smith returned to Ibrox in 2007 and a fantastic UEFA Cup run the following year was all the more distinguished because it was achieved with arguably the weakest Rangers side in two decades. Murray again stood down as chairman in 2009 and was replaced by Alastair Johnston. This was also the year that Smith secured the first of three successive league titles. His sides in this period may have been more dogged and determined than scintillating but they had the same will to win that characterised earlier Rangers teams.

During an interview in 2010, Smith confirmed the suspicions of many when he said the Lloyds Banking Group was running Rangers Football Club. The debt was still unnerving, even more so when added to the confirmation in April of that year that Her Majesty's Revenue and Customs (HMRC) was investigating the use of EBTS. It was reported that a bill for as much as £50m might be forthcoming. This case would be the subject of much speculation, based on little real knowledge, for another two years. This speculation had a detrimental effect on Sir David Murray's attempts to sell the club, something he was openly trying to do. In April 2011, a further tax liability of £2.8m was revealed, stemming from the use of a discounted option scheme, which some players were part of, between 1999 and 2003. The following month, after a protracted period of what was referred to at the time as due diligence, it was announced that Motherwell-born businessman Craig Whyte had purchased MIH's 85.3 per cent shareholding in Rangers for the nominal sum of £1. This went against the concerns of members of the board who had investigated Whyte and met him and his advisors on several occasions. A 15 page report outlining these concerns was prepared for Murray but didn't have the effect its authors desired. The deal was contingent on Whyte accepting any liability resulting from the First Tier Tax Tribunal which was hearing Rangers' appeal on the tax owing from the administration of the EBT scheme. He also undertook to settle the outstanding debt with the bank, which stood at £18m, provide £9.5m of new money for capital expenditure and player acquisition, and to pay the £2.8m owed to HMRC.

Whyte had an obscure business background, with few achievements of note that might have allowed interested observers to get a handle on him. The circumstances surrounding this transaction have yet to be revealed in their totality. It has been suggested that pressure was applied in favour of the sale by Lloyds Banking Group and former board members Paul Murray and Alastair Johnston have been among those calling for serious scrutiny of the actions of Donald Muir who they considered the bank's representative on the board of The Rangers Football Club PLC towards the end of the Murray era. At the time of writing, some of these matters are being investigated by Strathclyde Police and the liquidators BDO. It would later be revealed that Whyte had made a deal with Ticketus to pay off the outstanding £18m debt to Lloyds and his calamitous lack of genuine resources would eventually drag Rangers into the mire of an insolvency event.

On 14 February 2012, Rangers appointed Duff & Phelps as Administrators following a contest with HMRC at the Court of Session. It was revealed that HMRC had lodged a petition to force administration over the non-payment of PAYE and VAT since Whyte's takeover. For fans, the administration process seemed to have only two speeds, bewilderingly fast or frustratingly slow. Professor David Kinnon provides an expert analysis of the events and missed opportunities of this period in chapter I. He also tackles fundamental questions including whether insolvency was inevitable and, based on recent financial information, what the future might hold for Rangers. It was not only the fans who had to contend with a fluid and unpredictable situation. Prospective bidders vied with each other for the favour of the Administrators and supporters who often knew little or nothing about them. In chapter II Calvin Spence charts the ebbs and flows of this process which saw former unknowns become headline makers overnight. Stewart Franklin considers the role of social media in relation to the ownership contest, with key contributions from journalists and club figures who understood its integral role in shaping the story, in chapter III.

Among the corporate carnage, there was a simpler football grievance. In chapter IV, Colin Armstrong recalls the pain that was caused by the dismantling of a successful team. Few of the players opted to remain with the club as it began its journey back to the top from the basement of Scottish football; this was despite many being considered 'Rangers men'. The way these departures were conducted hurt many fans. Those who decided to stay were lauded as heroes and stalwarts but it was hard to avoid the conclusion that playing for Rangers was no longer the honour it had once been. With the departure of much of the playing squad, Ally McCoist assumed even more importance as a source of continuity.

It was a source of frustration to many Rangers fans that the Scottish football authorities often seemed content to act as the spanner in the works. Chris Graham outlines a series of bizarre decisions that weakened the position of the club in chapter V. In his second chapter (VI), he considers the friction between elements of the media on the one hand and the club and fans on the other. Rangers' fans were often given cause to believe that certain journalistic standards had become secondary to the need to play catch-up with a narrative shaped by new media. This was occasionally obvious in the form of simple pettiness but also in more serious forms such as prejudgement of guilt and disregard for known facts. On 12 June 2012, HMRC announced their intention to reject a Company Voluntary Arrangement (CVA) that would have seen an exit from administration agreed with the creditors. This came as a surprise as the Administrators had repeatedly implied that HMRC would be open to such an outcome despite precedent suggesting the opposite. Two days later, the assets of The Rangers Football Club PLC were purchased for £5.5m by a consortium fronted by Charles Green. The old company being placed into liquidation signalled the start of a period of intense confrontation between various stakeholders in Scottish football.

It was obvious that, for the time being at least, Rangers fans could only rely on each other. Duty and loyalty became the watchwords once again and, as Alasdair McKillop argues in chapter VII, it was the fans that helped to rebuild Rangers. In the process, it was demonstrated that there was much about the club worth celebrating. Any sense of siege mentality was secondary to the need to support the club – a rededication was called for. Estranged fans, such as Iain Duff writing in chapter VIII, suddenly fell in love with the club again as the excitement of the Souness era was rekindled by supporters queuing in huge numbers to buy season tickets

It became clear that the narrative spread by blogs such as *Rangers Tax Case* (RTC) was exerting a disproportionate influence on people's understanding of what was going on at Ibrox. Terms such as 'financial doping', 'cheating' and 'sporting integrity' became commonplace as the situation became morally overheated. At times, social media flirted with collapsing under the weight of all the grandstanding. The absence of important decisions from SPL Commissions and Tax Tribunals was no impediment to stating Rangers were guilty of something, probably everything, with absolute, self-satisfied authority. Rangers fans were expecting few favours from fans of other teams, but, in this atmosphere, even empathy seemed to be in short supply. As Gail Richardson discusses in chapter IX, the level of animosity directed at the club and fans was painful and even had the potential to strain relationships between close friends. John DC Gow argues that much of the hatred directed at the club was the result of it being falsely painted as the main source of sectarianism in Scotland, and he contends in chapter X that Rangers FC need to change that image by openly leading the anti-sectarian debate.

The time of spending big on players of questionable value should be truly over but how, then, does a club like Rangers remain successful? This is one of the many challenges facing the management team. At boardroom level, there is a need to maximise revenue streams to ensure the club remains on a sound financial footing. International markets look to be one potential source of growth but building a global profile for a Scottish football club is a daunting prospect. It is these issues and more that Ross E.J. Hendry tackles in chapter XI.

The legacy of this period for the fans remains to be seen but it is certainly desirable that it leads to a culture of activism and scrutiny, with the splits of the past rendered meaningless by what has been endured. David Edgar contends that this is certainly one possible outcome, while also believing that Rangers fans will adopt an uncompromising attitude towards the rest of Scottish football. Countering the effects of a long period of disenfranchisement will not be easy but neither are the fans powerless to shape the future of the club. *The Herald* journalist Richard Wilson concludes by arguing in chapter XIII that lessons must be learned and opportunities grasped, with fan ownership an apparently logical outcome of this period. In the meantime, those responsible for the financial and footballing fate of the club also need to consider what lessons can be learned from 2012 and the preceding years.

This is the story of how one of the most successful clubs in world football ended up in the Scottish Third Division and how some of the most loyal fans in the world defended it and helped it overcome unprecedented challenges.

W Stewart Franklin
John DC Gow
Chris Graham
Alasdair McKillop

CHAPTER I

From Crash to Cash... and beyond

DAVID KINNON

THROUGHOUT THE HISTORY of The Rangers Football Club, famous names have left their imprint. McNeil, Meiklejohn, Struth, Waddell, Greig, Gough and more inspire enduring respect for their great achievements. But not all names are remembered in such a positive light. One name in particular – Craig Whyte – has become notorious since the club was almost obliterated under his rule. Another name – Charles Green – sparks debate and arouses like and dislike, trust and distrust, gratitude and scepticism in equal measure. This chapter looks at the impact of these most recent names in the club's history, the financial crash and appraises the subsequent recovery.

The bare facts are simple. Whyte's acquisition by questionable means on 9 May 2011 set off a chain of events in 2011 and 2012 that propelled the club in a spiral towards disaster. Charles Green and a financial consortium created a new holding company, acquired the club, raised over £20m of fresh equity in challenging markets and saw stage one of the recovery completed by winning the Third Division championship of season 2012–13. At the time of writing Green has just stood down as Chief Executive of Rangers International Football Club PLC. The pot continues to boil.

Both before and during Rangers' financial crash, lurid and dramatic headlines became normal amongst broadcasters and media. These focused on the implications of financial difficulties, and were dominated by what became known as the Big Tax Case (BTC), with liberal allegations of 'cheating' aimed at the club, although in fact it was the victim rather than the perpetrator of corporate wrongdoing. Joint Administrators from Duff & Phelps encountered a severe examination of their performance, in the most difficult of circumstances – a Scottish institution humbled, fans that were angry and willing to mobilise all resources to save the club they loved. Contrary to popular predictive wisdom, the outcomes of proceedings involving HM Revenue & Customs (HMRC) and the Scottish Premier League were decided in the club's favour, although HMRC have given notice of an appeal, as discussed later in this chapter.

This saga has its roots as far back as the year 2000. Nine league championships in a row had been clinched by season 1996–7. A tenth proved beyond Walter Smith as manager and he left at the end of season 1997–8. With hindsight, the loss of the calm authority of Smith perhaps unshackled the chairman, Sir David Murray, to pursue success in the European Champions League through expensive player purchases. Walter Smith's astute signings, such as Brian Laudrup and Paul Gascoigne, were succeeded by more expensive purchases during Dick Advocaat's time as manager, the most expensive of all being the enigmatic Tore André Flo in November 2000 for a fee of £12m. Business plans were unrealistic. Had success been achieved in Europe the heavy expenditure on players would have been recouped from television revenues, prize money and other commercial sources. In the absence of such success, the economics of the domestic game in Scotland meant that Rangers could not sustain expenditure at that level.

On 30 March 2000, BBC Scotland reported that £53m in fresh share capital was being raised, with £32m to be invested by one of Sir David Murray's companies and £20m coming from Dave King. The latter had become wealthy through business activities in South Africa, although he was originally from Castlemilk in Glasgow. Mr King was quoted as saying:

> With a capital investment of this kind we believe Rangers can very quickly move to a new level.

The report also stated that:

> At the end of February, the club's bank borrowings stood at £48m, having invested £54.8m in players in the three financial periods up to June 1999.

On 16 January 2004, BBC Sport's website published an article entitled 'Murray takes Ibrox blame', which opened by stating:

> Rangers honorary chairman David Murray is shouldering the blame for the overspending that has led to the club's current financial plight. The Ibrox club are [sic] struggling with debts of around £65m leaving manager Alex McLeish little cash to strengthen his playing pool.

The article went on to report that John McClelland, chairman since 2002, and his team were well down the road with a three year plan to stabilise the club. By this time, Alex McLeish had succeeded Dick Advocaat as manager and, in his first full season of 2002–3, he delivered the domestic treble of Scottish Premier League (SPL) championship, Scottish Cup and Scottish League Cup. Austerity was the hallmark of the McLeish years, with hard-working players replacing those who were arguably more gifted.

By the time Walter Smith returned as manager in January 2007, assisted by Ally McCoist, his task was to downsize the squad through selling and releasing players. On 7 March 2009 the BBC Sport website reported that Rangers were offering their staff voluntary redundancy terms. The success of reaching the UEFA Cup in May 2008 was followed by failure to qualify for the UEFA Champions League at the beginning of the 2008–9 season. On 26 August 2009, only ten days after the League Championship flag had been unfurled at Ibrox, the BBC Sport website reported that Sir David Murray (as he was by then) had stood down as chairman in favour of Alastair Johnston, a senior executive of IMG Group based in the USA. On 29 August 2009, that website gave further information on Johnston's credentials: vice chairman of IMG Group, former chief operating officer of Arnold Palmer Enterprises and director of Rangers since 2004. Sir David Murray commented:

> I am delighted that Alastair Johnston has accepted the chairmanship. He is an internationally renowned and respected businessman and he will be an excellent servant to the club.

It is worth noting here that Alastair Johnston's association with Rangers had begun long before he became chairman. His knowledge of the club by the date of his appointment should have been thorough. Johnston himself explained the objectives of his role in another article on the BBC Sport website on 28 September 2009, which opened by saying:

> Rangers chairman Alastair Johnston has listed finding a new owner for the club and retaining the services of manager Walter Smith as his two main targets.

Without explaining exactly why, the report continued:

> Johnston's view is that by finding a suitable investor to buy [Sir David] Murray's shareholding, the club would be freed from servicing the heavy levels of debt necessitated by external financing.

Whatever Alastair Johnston imagined was his role, Walter Smith significantly qualified the task. According to BBC Sport's website on 29 October 2009, Smith stated that all of his players had been for sale since January 2009 and that Lloyds Banking Group PLC was effectively running the club, an idea quickly dismissed by the bank. The collapse of HBOS – who had been bankers for Rangers in the latter part of 2008 – when the global banking crisis came to a head, and the subsequent acquisition of HBOS by Lloyds, may have had an impact on the banking relationship which Rangers had previously enjoyed.

Little was made public of the chairman's efforts to attract a new investor, raise fresh equity or restructure the club's borrowings with Lloyds or otherwise. The reasonable conclusion is that he achieved little or nothing. The first ripples of what was to become an engulfing storm appeared in March 2010. News broke that a London-based property developer named Andrew Ellis was about to enter a period of due diligence, with debt then reported to be £30m. An independent committee of the Board was set up, comprising Alastair Johnston, John McClelland (who had remained a director since stepping down as chairman in 2004), Martin Bain (Chief Executive), Donald McIntyre (close business associate of Sir David Murray) and John Greig (legendary former team captain). In May 2010, Ellis reported himself to be optimistic that he would move closer to completing a takeover in that month, with a quoted figure of £33m. Although the analysis of how the money would be spent was never provided, he planned to wipe out the club's debt and to invest in new players. Walter Smith took public umbrage at Ellis' plan to offer him a new contract without apparently discussing the matter first. BBC Sport website reported on 15 June 2010 that the club was no longer for sale.

Certain aspects of that BBC Sport report were confusing to those familiar with the history of the matter. Firstly, debt was reported to be around £30m, having risen sharply from £10m the previous year. Earlier reports had not put bank debt as low as £10m.[1] Secondly, according to BBC Sport, Sir David Murray stated that Murray International Holdings Limited (MIH) had received interest in its controlling stake from a number of parties. No feverish interest had been reported previously. Thirdly, it was reported that:

> The board of directors of MIH therefore considers that the interests of stakeholders are presently best served by providing the football management team and board of directors with an opportunity to implement its business plan which is supported by Lloyds Banking Group.

It is very fair to ask why the support for the business plan seems to have ebbed away in a matter of months if not weeks, in favour of Lloyds Banking Group recovering its money by any means possible. Or maybe that was Lloyds' plan? On 15 June 2010, *The Scotsman* published an article headed 'Long-term player David Murray in no hurry to offload prized asset so close to his heart.' The article included the withering

---

[1] 'Rangers Move into Profit and Reduce Debt', BBC Sport Website, 22 September 2010

opinion that 'In reality the only ones showing interest were limping like mangy dogs towards Ibrox'.

Undeterred by the unflattering description, or perhaps unaware of the mangy march, Andrew Ellis re-surfaced in November 2010 with Craig Whyte. No mange was evident within a BBC Sport website report dated 18 November 2010, which said:

> Whyte, a 39-year-old millionaire who was raised in Motherwell and is a lifelong Rangers fan, is now based in London... Ellis, who was involved in a previous attempt to buy Rangers, and Whyte would invest major sums if the takeover of the Scottish Champions goes ahead.

Any initial scepticism was surely allayed by the further revelation within the article which said:

> Venture capitalist Whyte began in business at the age of 19 by establishing a plant hire firm, and has since expanded into security services and office cleaning.

This article included a statement by Stephen Smith, then chairman of the Rangers Supporters Trust, which probably reflected the position of many fans and read:

> I think we had concerns about the viability of Mr Ellis's [previous] bid in terms of the due diligence process which went on. But our understanding is that this is a completely different animal and we don't have the same concerns about the viability of Mr Whyte's company or the organisations that he is involved in.

Craig Whyte's business history received little scrutiny from the press at that time. He later denied that he was a millionaire, and was revealed to have been involved with a number of failed businesses. His conduct as a director of a company which entered into liquidation had led to a seven-year ban from being a director in 2000, imposed by the Insolvency Service under the Company Directors' Disqualification Act 1986.

Rumours of discord within the Ibrox boardroom swirled around the activities of two directors named Donald Muir and Mike McGill, who came to be regarded by their fellow directors, rightly or wrongly, as acting in the interests of Lloyds Banking Group, and not necessarily in the interests of Rangers. The temperature was cranked up when, on 1 April 2011, Alastair Johnston stated it was a possibility that Rangers could go bust if the BTC were to be lost. To many Rangers fans, the existence of a life-threatening tax case was news indeed. Later in this chapter the nature of HMRC's allegations and the actual basis of the HMRC assessments will be examined in detail. For the time being, it is worth noting that this should not have been news to John McClelland, who was chairman in 2002 when Rangers became involved with the Employee Remuneration Trust operated by Murray Group, nor to Alastair Johnston, who had been appointed a director by the time HMRC began to raise queries on the Trust in 2005. The existence of this potential liability may have increased Sir David Murray's desire to sell his interest in Rangers, and may have been an equal and opposite disincentive to any potential purchaser.

In May 2011, all was dazzlingly resolved. Craig Whyte acquired Sir David Murray's shareholding for £1; the debt to Lloyds Banking Group was settled at the negotiated figure of £18m; in terms of the share purchase agreement, Whyte undertook to make £25m available to fund transfers at the rate of £5m per season. By winning the Scottish Premier League, Walter Smith achieved the feat of winning three league titles in a row in two separate spells as manager. What in the garden could be rosier?

The acquisition prompts tough questions. What was Craig Whyte's source of funds? From where did he obtain the sum of £18m to settle the amount due to Lloyds Banking Group? By what means was he able to acquire the security of Lloyds Banking Group over substantial property assets? Legal proceedings provide the answers.

A Judgement was handed down on Friday 5 April 2013[2] relating to the action by Ticketus to recover money from Craig Whyte on the basis that he fraudulently obtained certain sums. The key facts are as follows:

- The operations of Ticketus are carried out by Octopus Investment limited which owns Ticketus. Ticketus has no employees.

- Ticketus buys tickets at a discount.

- Ticketus charges a fee for arranging the transaction.

- Ticketus charges interest on the amount they pay to buy the tickets.

- The seller sells the tickets at face value and pays that to Ticketus.

- Phil Betts entered into negotiations with Ticketus in October 2010. That is a full month before Andrew Ellis resurfaced in companionship with Craig Whyte.

- In October 2010, Craig Whyte signed a 'Term Sheet'. A Term Sheet sets out all of the main details: amount relating to buying

---

2 'In the High Court of Justice Chancery Division. Claim No: HC12F03282'

the tickets; fees; interest rate; means of repayment. Again, this is considerably before the interest of Ellis and Whyte in acquiring Sir David Murray's holding in Rangers was made public.

- The Term Sheet approved, in principle, the sum of £20 million worth of tickets.

- On 16 December 2010, a Directors' Questionnaire was sent to Phil Betts for completion by Craig Whyte.

- By 28 February 2011 this had still not been completed by Whyte. It was supplied on that day, unsigned, as he said he had no access to a scanner.

- The Directors' Questionnaire specifically asked for information on past disqualification as a director. Whyte answered the question 'No'. He had in fact been disqualified in June 2000 for a period of seven years in relation to the liquidation of a company named Vital UK Limited in respect of his 'misfeasance, breach of duty and negligence'.

- The deal was completed on 9 May 2011 when the first amount was advanced. A second amount was advanced in September 2011.

- Ticketus claimed in effect that Whyte had deceived them by failing to declare his past disqualification as a director. Ticketus claimed £26,711,856.81 plus costs of £541,003.

- The Judge found in favour of Ticketus. Judgement was entered in the sum of £17,683,338 and the amount in respect of costs will be subject to an enquiry.

So in May 2011, Craig Whyte appears to have acquired control of Rangers by deceiving a financial institution into advancing millions of pounds to purchase rights to season tickets which he had no entitlement to sell.

Whyte wasted no time in appointing fresh corporate advisers or in making key executive appointments. Phil Betts, touted as a turnaround expert, was appointed finance director. As will be seen, he had a pivotal role in the negotiations with Ticketus by which Whyte obtained funds to settle the Lloyds Banking Group debt. Ali Russell, who was sometime head of business development of the Scottish Rugby Union in flourishing times, was recruited as Head of Marketing. Gordon Smith, ex-Rangers player, players' agent and pundit, was appointed Director of Football.

No time was wasted in Europe either. Early exits from both the UEFA Champions League and Europa League preceded elimination from the

Scottish League Cup. Whatever financial plans were under considera-
tion for the forthcoming season – and it is by no means certain that there
were any – were in tatters. The sale of the club's star striker, Croatian
international Nikica Jelavić, to Leicester City for £7m was not completed before the transfer window closed. Matters went from disquietingly
bad to alarmingly worse. It became public knowledge that in respect of
a tax liability, sheriff officers had arrived at Ibrox to seize certain assets on
the instructons of HMRC. However, it is odd that a turnaround expert
such as Phil Betts would be inexperienced in handling threats of such
appearances, which, in fairness to HMRC, are usually exercised as a power
of last resort. No time was wasted in failing to complete the audited
financial statements for the year to 30 June 2011, or in failing to deal
with the PLUS Market regulator over the delay in submitting these in
accordance with the PLUS Market regulations. Again, it seems odd that a
turnaround expert in a finance director post would not see bringing
compliance up to date as a key task. It seems even more odd that an
entrepreneur of Craig Whyte's assumed experience would be equally lax
in such filings.

It did not become public until much later that Whyte had also sold 16
shares in the company which operates Arsenal Football Club. Difficult
financial circumstances can dictate that hard financial choices have to be
made. This includes the ruthless identification of surplus assets. Fatal to
Whyte's reputation amongst many Rangers fans was the decision to sell
these shares, which were iconic of the historic relationship between Rangers
and Arsenal. The sale was conducted through a stockbroking firm of
which Whyte was Company Secretary and which was placed into insolvency proceedings under the rules of the Financial Services Authority.

In late January 2012, Andrew Ellis replaced Phil Betts on the board of
The Rangers Football Club PLC. It is not clear what appreciable difference
this change was intended to make to the quality of financial mismanagement from which the club was suffering. In the wake of failure to remit
PAYE and National Insurance amounts, HMRC chose to pursue recovery
through the Courts. Persons who have been involved in insolvency proceedings will recognise a pattern of events. Tension builds to the date of
appointment as frantic efforts to avoid insolvency proceedings continue.
On appointment, there is a feeling akin to bereavement as the reality
sinks in. The appointment takers, in this case the Joint Administrators,
arrive with their staff to address all employees and to explain the likely
course of events. Attitudes often sour when it becomes clear that redundancies will follow swiftly, and attitudes harden when the staff of the

appointment taker take possession of everything, seek explanations and analysis, and may demonstrate little understanding of the business to which they have been appointed.

Given that a partner in Duff & Phelps named David Grier had a long-standing friendship with Donald Muir, the former director who allegedly provided the board's link to Lloyds Banking Group, and given that Duff & Phelps was a firm of Craig Whyte's choosing, it is not at all surprising that conspiracy theories flourished. Although Whyte's corporate track record, including his disqualification as a director, indicated familiarity with insolvency proceedings, it seems that he may have miscalculated on this occasion. It was Whyte himself who talked up liability under the BTC to levels of liability of £75m and higher. Without having that liability at such a level, it was debatable whether Rangers Football Club PLC was actually insolvent. The level of HMRC indebtedness gave it a whip-hand in proceedings which they were never likely to relinquish.

Let's pause here to look at the findings of the First Tier Tax Tribunal (FTTT) to understand the nature of the events which gave rise to the liability under the BTC. The FTTT sat for 17 days and the documented decision runs to 145 pages.[3] The first 59 pages contain the record of proceedings, findings of fact, findings of law and the majority decision reached by Messrs Mure and Rae. The remaining 86 pages contain the dissenting opinion of Dr Poon. This anonymised version contains a list of 15 witnesses generally named as colours: Mr Red, Mrs Crimson. Persons referred to were given place names: Mr Inverness, Mrs Bedford.

As this matter remains subject to appeal by HMRC no analysis of the reasons for the FTTT's decision will be offered. Only the facts as established will be considered, along with the Tribunal's judgement. The FTTT was concerned with other companies of the Murray Group, and not only Rangers. Before the Employee Remuneration Trust, discretionary bonuses were paid by Rangers to players. The law changed with effect from April 2011 to ensure that 'disguised remuneration' schemes such as Employee Benefit Trusts could not operate to reduce tax or national insurance contributions and the use of the Trust ceased.[4] The Trust was established in

---

3 Anonymised Form of the Decision [2012] UK FTT 692 (TC) reference TC02372 Appeal Number SC/3113-3117/2009 – First Tier Tribunal Tax Chamber – Murray Group Holdings and Others Appellants – The Commissioners for Her Majesty's Revenue and Customs – Respondents – Tribunal Judge: Mr Kenneth Mure QC; Dr Heidi Poon, CA, CTA, PhD; S A Rae, LLB, WS

4 http://www.hmrc.gov.uk/employers/employee-benefit-trusts.htm

the year 2000 for senior executives of the Murray Group. In the year 2001 it was extended to Rangers for payment of senior executives and football players. The mechanism of the Trust was set out at paragraph 103 of the Judgement, broadly as follows:

- Payments were made into a main trust. Sub-trusts were created for each individual.
- As part of contractual arrangements, players entered into a contract and the club gave a letter of undertaking to recommend the player for inclusion within the Trust arrangements. The letter of undertaking became disparagingly known as a 'side-letter'.
- Money paid into the main trust was allocated to the relevant sub-trust.
- Under a 'Letter of Wishes', the player named the beneficiaries of the sub-trust, such as his wife and family members. The player was not the ultimate beneficiary: those nominated by him were.
- The player was entitled to borrow from the sub-trust. Here is the factor which the press did not seem to report. The player remained liable to the sub-trust for the money borrowed and his estate became liable after his death.
- Payments made under these trust arrangements were fully disclosed within the relevant financial statements by Rangers.

In paragraphs 232 and 233 the findings of law are set out, broadly as follows:

- The principal trust deed was valid and continues.
- The sub-trusts were valid and continue.
- The sums advanced to players were made 'in pursuance of discretionary powers and remain recoverable and represent debts on their estates'.
- The sums advanced into the trust arrangements were not held at any time absolutely or unreservedly for or to the order of the particular employee.
- Accordingly, the assessments fall to be reduced substantially. The Appeal was agreed in principle and the parties were expected to settle sums due for the limited number of cases (where trust arrangements had not been properly complied with).

In other words, the evidence of witnesses generally regarded by the FTTT as reliable, led by expert counsel over 17 days, resulted in Rangers' liability under the BTC being virtually eliminated. Unless HMRC win their appeal against the Tribunal's decision, the forever open question will be 'If HMRC had not pursued their action, or if the Tribunal's decision had been delivered earlier, would Administration or Liquidation have resulted?'

Sadly, the answer to that would appear to be yes. It was not the BTC which gave rise to the HMRC petition to appoint an Administrator. It was the failure of the Craig Whyte regime to remit PAYE and National Insurance contributions throughout their tenure which lay at the root of HMRC's petition.[5] For a different reason the answer would also be yes. Whyte never had the funds to ensure Rangers had sufficient working capital. Bluntly, in my opinion, Rangers traded whilst insolvent and from the day Whyte achieved control, formal insolvency was a ticking time bomb.

The race to the insolvency wire was almost a dead heat. Craig Whyte gave Notice of Intention to Appoint to the Courts on 13 February 2012 and HMRC presented their application to appoint an Administrator on 14 February 2012. After some legal wrangling, Paul Clark and David Whitehouse of Duff & Phelps were appointed Joint Administrators of Rangers Football Club PLC with HMRC's consent. Even that had an element of farce. The documents presented to the Court overlooked the fact that at one time the club had been appointed as an authorised representative under the prevailing financial services legislation. No consent to formal insolvency proceedings had been obtained from the Financial Services Authority. Thus, although the appointment was effective from 14 February 2012, the Court Order was not actually granted until 19 March 2012 when the error had been rectified.

The Administration became really messy and the Joint Administrators came under heavy criticism for their handling of certain matters. For the sake of clarity it is worth pointing out that the Joint Administrators were appointed to Rangers Football Club PLC. That is, they were appointed Administrators over the company which operated the club and owned the business of the club and its substantial property assets. Although they received criticism, much of it was harsh and from people who seemingly understood little of insolvency matters. With hindsight, it seems clear that the Administrators took control with a view to achieving an early sale of the business, most likely to a group of individuals colloquially known as the Blue Knights. It is fair to say that the Joint Administrators may have approached matters differently on a number of fronts:

---

[5] 'Rangers plunge into administration over £75m tax demand', Mail Online, 14 February 2012

1   On the negotiation of temporary salary reductions for the playing staff, in exchange for reductions in the amount for which they could be sold by the club in the forthcoming summer. Coupled with the shift from Administration into Liquidation, this meant that many experienced and talented players walked away free of any transfer fee payable to Rangers.

2   On the reduction in the establishment, including redundancies. Paragraph 4.2 of the First Report to Creditors dated 5 April 2012 discloses that at the date of appointment, 326 staff were employed, including 67 players. Simple arithmetic shows that 259 members of staff were employed in other operations. It is hard to imagine that the club requires this many people in other operations. Perhaps reductions in non-playing staff ought to have been made at the time.

3   On the production of an Information Memorandum, to include a somewhat sharper outline of the assumptions underlying the club's prospects and thus of the accompanying financial projections of trading in the medium term.

4   On the question of selling the club, time afforded to the Blue Knights acted to suppress bid values in the nature of a Dutch auction rather than stimulate a competitive sale process. Although the market was well tested, it is arguable that a higher price ought to have been obtained. Perhaps a more clinical approach to the sale would have resulted in the sale to a properly funded and credible bidder.

5   On the construction of the Company Voluntary Arrangement (CVA) proposal. Commercially it stood little chance of acceptance, given the amount of funds to be injected. The highest bid, which proposed to make available £8.5m if the CVA proposal were accepted by creditors, was inadequate to secure the agreement of HMRC. The prospective recovery by creditors was minimal.

6   On the admission of the full estimated amount of the HMRC liability taking into account the amount then still subject to the First Tier Tax Tribunal. Perhaps court direction could have been obtained so that HMRC could have voted on the FTTT claim at a nominal figure of £1, with the amount finally settled by the Tribunal ranking in full for payment.

7   On the treatment of the shareholding, amounting to 85 per cent of shares in issue, held by Craig Whyte. Again, court direction may have been sought to take control of the voting power of the

Whyte shares in order to prevent him from blocking a deal, and to subsequently re-structure the shareholding by converting it into a class of share capital with negligible value going forward. Given that he paid the sum of £1 for his shareholding it is arguable that the shares were worthless.

As is usual in insolvency proceedings, the prospect of a sale of assets at a discounted or distressed value attracted a number of persons with no discernible interest in Rangers as a club, but with interest in the property asset as a redevelopment opportunity. In fact, the Duff & Phelps Interim Report dated 12 July 2012 was a well written and comprehensive document, covering in a very satisfactory manner all of the key matters handled by the Joint Administrators to that date. Section 5 of that document sets out the process of dealing with four bidders, a number which subsequently rose to six.

That section included a number of formidable factors which made construction of a bid virtually impossible, far less a bid which was 'unconditional' or one which included a non-refundable deposit in exchange for a period of exclusivity. The factors requiring clarification included:

- The status of the Ticketus agreement.
- The manner of dealing with Craig Whyte as shareholder.
- The likelihood of success of a CVA proposal, and in particular the attitude of HMRC.
- The extent of SFA and SPL sanctions.
- The transfer of memberships of SPL and SFA respectively. (At that stage no possibility other than that of continuing as an SPL member was in contemplation.)
- The possibility of participation in Europe, given the failure to produce audited financial statements and payment of all payroll-related taxes to the satisfaction of UEFA.

Not all of the bidders are clearly identified within the report and it is unhelpful to guess at their identities. Each was regarded with extreme cynicism by Rangers fans, and perhaps rightly so in the light of the recent past. Ironically, the Rangers fans welcomed and supported the Blue Knights led by Paul Murray and joined by Brian Kennedy, whose previous sporting investment interests were not conspicuously successful in sporting terms – Stockport County (football) and Sale Sharks (rugby union).

The report referred to Bill Miller by name. His bid was unworkable in terms of UK law. He attempted to impose a 'segregated asset' approach on the problem, taking 'good' assets which the club would use as the basis of operation, leaving questionable assets and liabilities to be dealt with through a formal insolvency process. His bid was ultimately withdrawn.

Bill Ng from Singapore was not named. His bid was understood to be for the business and assets, and would not have involved a CVA. His view was perhaps clearest in its thinking. With hindsight, his approach may well have been the least painful way of moving forward, although any use of the word liquidation provoked howls from supporters.

The Blue Knights seemed to be in pole position time and again, but for some reason could not get the very basics right. There was never a written agreement amongst the Blue Knights capable of underpinning a successful bid. It is not known if a formal and comprehensive bid was ever submitted or whether perhaps a letter of offer, scant in detail, or telephone conversations alone held the substance of the bid.

Shortly before the date of the Meeting of Creditors to consider the CVA, Charles Green exploited the indecision of the Blue Knights by tabling a bid conditional upon the acceptance by creditors of a CVA, plus a bid to acquire the business, history and assets should the CVA fail. At a stroke, even at what some may have perceived as an undervaluation, Charles Green provided the Joint Administrators with a workable option. When HMRC finally and at short notice informed the Joint Administrators that they would be rejecting the CVA, they had a backstop position. The CVA proposal was rejected and the sale to Charles Green took place.

Perhaps the most bizarre of the bids came from none of the above, and may not have formally existed. When it became clear that Charles Green was in pole position, and that the Blue Knights had tabled nothing of acceptable substance over months, a fresh group appeared on the scene, fronted by Walter Smith and backed by a Scottish entrepreneur, Jim McColl. By the time of their appearance, the CVA meeting date was set and for statutory reasons would not be cancelled or postponed. Was it possible for McColl's group to have trumped Green? By appearing as a creditor or on behalf of a creditor at the Meeting of Creditors, they could have suggested radical amendments to the CVA, including an increase in the amount of cash to be subscribed if the CVA were successful, or amendments to the list of Excluded Assets per the CVA so that SPL prize money and SPL media income would have been available to the creditors. This would have meant that the Joint Administrators would have had no alternative but to adjourn the meeting for 14 days.

Then, in the adjournment, some serious negotiation with the Joint Administrators, or even with Charles Green, could have taken place.

Whatever advice Jim McColl's group obtained, they appear to have completely missed that trick and became irrelevant.

Thus, a certainty of sorts was achieved. Charles Green completed his deal and the old company proceeded into liquidation. Complete certainty remained elusive. A summer of cliff-hanging intensity emerged, with the intransigence of SPL and SFA representatives noticeable. Attempts to rehabilitate the club within Scottish football were anything but well-received, other than by the Scottish Football League (SFL).

Charles Green proved himself to be a real champion of the Rangers cause, standing up for the club's rights in a way that his predecessors had not. He accomplished membership of the SFL, albeit by entry into the Third Division, the fourth and lowest tier of Scottish league football. He never quite won over all of the fans, undermined as he was by repeated claims of links to Craig Whyte (largely circulated by Whyte himself).[6] Heavy doubt also surrounded his ability to introduce funds and yet he succeeded in raising more than £20m by means of an initial public offering of shares admitted to listing on the Alternative Investment Market before the end of 2012, just as he said he would. The AIM document produced bold initiatives for the development of the club, the acquisition and development of land surrounding Ibrox Stadium, fresh retail and sponsorship partners on improved financial terms and the objective of a return to playing football at the highest European levels. Sadly for Charles Green, his clumsiness in public relations led to one mistake from which he would not recover, involving remarks concerning his colleague Imran Ahmad.

So after the crash and raising the cash, what lies ahead for Rangers? Does new-found financial security translate into ongoing financial and operating stability? Can the bloated, overspending organisation which Craig Whyte acquired and ran into the ground turn itself into the model of operating efficiency, living within its means as it relentlessly achieves success on the pitch alongside success in the city? Can this board display the tough-minded financial discipline required to eliminate past excesses and prudently manage resources well into the future? The very existence of such questions brings unease to the minds of Rangers fans. The convulsions which have recently surrounded the board make these questions almost impossible to answer.

Having the financial heart of the club beating strongly is just as

---

[6] 'I brought Charles Green in to buy Rangers', BBC News Website, 17 October 2012

important as seeing an end to the factionalism which has blighted the past. Decisiveness and effectiveness are not words which spring to mind when considering past board performance. Successive chairmen have not succeeded in mentoring a prosperous, progressive club. 'Real Rangers men' have proved a handicap to progress as often as not, both from inside and outside the club. Recent rumours of willingness to invest are evidence of a self-importance not fulfilled by positive action.

Walter Smith, chairman at the time of writing, has a sizeable task in leading a board which will oversee proper corporate governance, drive domestic and European competitiveness and maintain the confidence of the fans over the handling of the club's financial and external affairs.

Craig Mather, as interim Chief Executive at the time of writing, has much to prove. Largely unknown to the Rangers fans at the date of joining the board as sporting director, he is reported to have been anonymous around Murray Park, the epicentre of football operations. According to media reports, his background in football is limited. Perhaps his business experience will equip him to meet the strategic challenges of building the development infrastructure covering coaching, scouting and transfer policy. He will be measured too against his ability to defend the club's interests in the ongoing, never-ending SPL-inspired league restructuring debate. Whatever faults Charles Green may have had, he held no fear of the SPL and its Chief Executive Neil Doncaster, nor of the SFA and its Chief Executive, Stewart Regan.

Brian Stockbridge as finance director emerges from the Green era as a very competent individual. Not a flamboyant man, he portrays a serious-ness and grasp of detail which the club requires. His decision to stay or to go after the departure of Charles Green may yet be the most telling of all in the long run.

The past 18 months have been difficult beyond the imaginable, testing almost beyond the reasonable and managed to the point of impos-sible. The forthcoming season will severely test all of those involved with Rangers and will again no doubt see the tremendous willingness of the fans to do all that they can to support and sustain the club they undoubtedly love. The next three to five years will determine whether Rangers have come through this torrid period as a cleansing prelude to future glory, or as a convulsive harbinger of no great revival.

Time will tell.

CHAPTER II

Rescuing Rangers:
From Whyte to Green

CALVIN SPENCE

TUESDAY 14 FEBRUARY 2012 is a date that will not be remembered fondly by Rangers supporters. Valentine's Day it may have been, but there were no expressions of fondness that day; no romantic trysts but, rather, a cold, dispassionate, matter-of-fact meeting between lawyers, tax men and representatives of Scotland's most historic footballing institution in the unwelcoming atmosphere of Her Majesty's Court of Session in Edinburgh.

After a three hour courtroom battle with Her Majesty's Revenue and Customs (HMRC), and much against HMRC's wishes, the Court of Session appointed Duff & Phelps to act as Administrators of The Rangers Football Club PLC. No sooner had Administrators Paul Clark and David Whitehouse settled into their new Ibrox home, than they revealed that HMRC had lodged a petition to take Rangers into administration over the non-payment of around £9m in PAYE and VAT under Craig Whyte. Former owner Sir David Murray, who sold his majority shareholding to Whyte in May 2011, expressed surprise and disappointment[1] that the club had been plunged into administration, although he avoided any reference to the latter years under his stewardship that had made Rangers a prime target for the dishonesty of Craig Whyte.

Back then, little did fans realise just how prominent a part HMRC would play in the fortunes of Rangers Football Club, and how the club's many opponents would exploit, distort, and even lie about our alleged tax liability. At that time, all eyes were on the Scottish Football Association (SFA) and the Scottish Premier League (SPL). What would they do, and what sanctions would they impose? Stewart Regan, the Chief Executive of the SFA said:

---

[1] 'Rangers in crisis: Sir David Murray "surprised" at decision to enter administration and admits he has no right to buy back club', *Daily Record*, 15 February 2012

> It is now incumbent on the club to enter into discussions with the appointed administrator to find a resolution on behalf of their creditors and for the Scottish Premier League to apply sanctions in accordance with their regulations.[2]

It would not take us long to learn what he really meant when he made the statement 'to apply sanctions in accordance with their regulations'.

Rangers were docked ten points by the SPL, leaving them 14 points behind Celtic in a title race that was no longer winnable. Just a few days later, on 17 February, fans were given a foretaste of things to come when the SFA launched an independent inquiry into the activities of Rangers and, specifically, whether Craig Whyte was a fit and proper person to own Rangers Football Club or, indeed, to hold any position in the Scottish game. The inquiry, which was to be headed by Lord Nimmo Smith (who would later re-emerge during the very public witch-hunt relating to Rangers' use of Employee Benefit Trusts), was launched in circumstances that puzzled and perplexed many observers, given that it happened some ten months after Craig Whyte had bought Rangers at the beginning of May 2011. 'Why did the SFA not carry out these checks ten months ago?' was the question being asked by many Rangers fans. The print and broadcast media turned a blind eye to that particular question, and the many others this raised about the SFA and its Chief Executive. Yet that simple question would pale into insignificance beside the vindictiveness that would characterise the actions of many individuals and organisations in the weeks and months ahead as Scottish football was plunged into crisis.

The sanctions alluded to by Stewart Regan were swiftly imposed, and the loss of our 2012 Champions League place was quickly followed by confirmation of a three year ban from European football with the inevitable loss of invaluable revenue. Thereafter, the sanctions followed thick and fast, with a £160,000 fine, the imposition of what turned out to be a legally unenforceable registration embargo (which meant the club could not adequately replace the 20 or so first team squad players it was to lose), the seizure of prize money and the withholding of substantial monies properly due to the club from player transfers.

Only a few short days later, the *Daily Record*, in an early glimpse of what was to come, announced after our 1-0 home defeat to Kilmarnock:

> Rangers don't walk away? It's a pity someone forgot to tell Craig Whyte because the man who has dumped this club into the hands of the

---

[2] 'Statement on Rangers FC entering administration', Scottish Football Association website, 14 February 2012

administrators was nowhere to be seen on Saturday when this crisis-torn club of his appeared, at least, to be hitting rock-bottom.[3]

What then followed was two weeks of intense, and often malicious, speculation about the imminent demise of our club, during which Rangers fans across the globe were effectively cut adrift and isolated. Anxious, worried and bereft of sympathy, we could do nothing but stand helplessly and witness the club's ignominious descent into crisis. Rudderless, leaderless, and wholly dependent upon Paul Clark and David Whitehouse of Duff & Phelps, we grasped at every straw and every snippet of information with hope and optimism. When Clark and Whitehouse announced that their work could be completed within a month and Rangers might compete in Europe next season, fans believed, perhaps naively, that our prospects were not as bleak as everyone had predicted.

However, the optimism of Clark and Whitehouse was quickly dashed, and the possibility that Rangers could still be in administration at the start of the next SPL campaign became a real concern for fans. March brought news that the SPL had launched another investigation, this time into allegations that Rangers had made undisclosed payments to players. This new investigation followed claims by former Rangers director Hugh Adam that some payments to players had not been included in the contracts registered with the SPL.[4] His allegations were a veritable godsend to those who were waiting to pounce on Rangers and eager to exaggerate and inflate his claims in articles and broadcasts which seemed designed to inflict maximum damage on the club.

All thoughts of verifying the accuracy of Adam's claims or awaiting the outcome of the First Tier Tax Tribunal (or the Big Tax Case, as it rapidly came to be known) were hastily discarded in the rush to condemn Rangers and moralise about 'sporting integrity'. It wasn't long before the football authorities succumbed to the clamour for retribution against Rangers. In a statement shortly after the Hugh Adam interview the SPL announced:

> The SPL board has instructed an investigation into the alleged non-disclosure to the SPL of payments made by or on behalf of Rangers FC to players since 1 July 1998.[5]

---

3 Keith Jackson, 'Chairman Craig Whyte goes AWOL as Rangers slump to Killie defeat', *Daily Record*, 20 February 2012

4 John McGarry, 'A new twist in Rangers controversy: Club accused of misleading SFA on secret deals', *Daily Mail*, 2 March 2012

5 'SPL Statement', Scottish Premier League website, 5 March 2012

With this statement, the SPL set in motion one of the most disreputable episodes in the history of Scottish football, and one that would tarnish the reputation of the SFA, SPL and the Scottish media. That, however, was in the future, and the immediate problem for the Administrators, and Rangers fans everywhere, was not the investigations ordered by the SFA and the SPL but the urgent need to find a new owner.

The emergence of the Blue Knights consortium at the beginning of March brought optimism that the club could, and would, be saved by Rangers men with the necessary money, clout and business acumen. Fans were given a further boost with the announcement from Duff & Phelps that they had received several additional bids for the club, including one from Brian Kennedy, the Scottish owner of English rugby union club Sale Sharks; one from a group based in Chicago backed by American millionaire Bill Miller and another headed by Singaporean businessman Bill Ng. Andy Kerr of the Rangers Supporters Assembly said:

> We would like the answer to basic questions: who are you and why do you want to buy Rangers? We have got to have confidence in this. We get bits and pieces and it would be helpful if we could put the pieces of the jigsaw together. So we would like to know who is in the race and on what basis, we want to know who is bidding to get the club out on a CVA and who wants to liquidate. We would like to have a discussion about their plans.[6]

As weeks turned into agonising months, Rangers fans would ask the same questions over and over again, as bid after bid failed. As each suitor came and went, optimism turned slowly and inexorably to anxiety and pessimism.

The Blue Knights, led by former Rangers director Paul Murray and supported by the Rangers Supporters Assembly, the Rangers Supporters Association and the Rangers Supporters Trust, moved quickly to submit their bid to secure the club and offer fans the opportunity to invest. Murray also revealed they had entered into an arrangement with Ticketus in their bid for ownership. Confidence was high that these Rangers men, in collaboration with a major creditor, would quickly secure the club. Explaining his reasons for involving them, Murray reasoned that Ticketus had a 'complete alignment of interest' with his group and wanted to see Rangers survive and prosper. He added:

> Ticketus' preference remains being part of a solution that brings financial stability to the Club. We are confident that the Consortium's bid is in

---

[6] 'Blue Knights first to put in their 'best and final bid' ', *Daily Record*, 4 April 2012

the best interests of the Club, its fans and creditors by guaranteeing the
future of Rangers and ending this period of uncertainty for the Club.[7]

Timely and welcome as the Blue Knights bid undoubtedly was, the
immediate crisis continued unabated, whilst the Administrators conducted talks with representatives of the club's many employees in order to
avoid damaging redundancies. Discussions took place with Ally McCoist,
his management team and the playing staff, while PFA Scotland chief
executive Fraser Wishart travelled back and forth to the Murray Park
training complex in an attempt to broker an arrangement.

As the end of March slowly approached, Duff & Phelps announced a
court hearing to challenge the Ticketus contract with Craig Whyte. Ticketus
had paid the shamed owner £24.4m for a season ticket deal that he subsequently used to pay off the £18m bank debt that he had pledged to
settle himself.[8] The presiding judge, Lord Hodge, ruled the company
had no security over the assets of Rangers and was a simple creditor with
the same rights as others owed money by the club. The initial optimism
over the Blue Knights marriage with Ticketus was suddenly cast into
doubt, and informed sources were predicting that the partnership would
quickly disintegrate.

Amidst the gathering gloom, a welcome ray of sunshine illuminated
Ibrox Stadium on Sunday 25 March when Rangers put the old enemy
to the sword in a thrilling 3–2 league encounter that prevented Celtic
clinching the title in Rangers' back yard. Sone Aluko scored a stunning
individual goal, and second half goals from Andy Little and Lee Wallace
spoiled the east-enders planned party, putting their title celebrations on
hold and sending a stunned Celtic support away empty-handed.

As April dawned and spring rapidly approached, a new owner seemed
as far away as ever. The optimism that followed the club's improbable
victory over Celtic rapidly faded as the *Daily Record* heaped further misery
on an impatient Rangers support with its 16 April headline, 'Rangers in
crisis: Blue Knights Consortium concede defeat in bid to buy Ibrox club'.
As some anticipated, Ticketus had reviewed their decision to partner
Murray's Blue Knights consortium and it was alleged they had been holding secret negotiations with Asian bidder Bill Ng in the hope of clawing
back more of their missing millions. In a statement, Ticketus said:

---

7 23 March 2012 Statement Response to court ruling, www.ticketus.co.uk
8 'Rangers owner Craig Whyte considering gifting shares to supporters', *The
   Independent*, 22 February 2012

Following extensive discussions with the Blue Knights, led by Paul Murray, Ticketus today confirms that it has withdrawn from the Blue Knights Consortium after it was unable to finalise satisfactory terms of agreement for its investors with the Blue Knights around restructuring its ticket purchase agreement.[9]

To add to the disappointment following the Blue Knights temporary withdrawal from the bidding process, fans then discovered that Brian Kennedy's latest offer for the club had been rejected by Duff & Phelps. They said his verbal offer was invalid and 'would not be capable of acceptance'. The roller coaster was plunging downward yet again.

As the Blue Knights and Brian Kennedy exited the stage (albeit temporarily), Singaporean Bill Ng and American millionaire Bill Miller, who had earlier unveiled his plans for an £11.2m bid for Rangers, were preparing for a showdown. Ng enthusiastically announced that he wanted to see Rangers 'make history rather than be history' and pledged to maintain the club's heritage. But as his dealings with Ticketus became public knowledge, fans began to wonder if he was just another hard-nosed businessman interested only in money and a positive return on his investment. It wasn't long before the question became irrelevant when, within days of announcing his bid, Ng had sensationally withdrawn. Whilst stating he had become 'increasingly uncomfortable and frustrated with the process of dealing with Duff & Phelps'[10], he also claimed there was no guarantee that his group would acquire Craig Whyte's 85 per cent shareholding even if they agreed a price. But the clincher for Ng appeared to be the demand from Ticketus for an additional £7.5m on top of the £10m they had reportedly agreed upon.

As Ng exited the process, Bill Miller found himself centre-stage as the only bidder left in the field. The beginning of May heralded the announcement by Duff & Phelps that Miller had been awarded 'preferred bidder' status, despite the fact (later disclosed) that he had not paid the £500,000 exclusivity fee which had been requested.

Never missing a trick, the *Daily Record* scented scandal and, perhaps, a juicy, salacious story in Miller's private life. The newspaper quickly dispatched journalist Mark McGivern to Tennessee to dig the dirt on Miller, and the story subsequently published on 5 May 2012 brought the rather sordid headline: 'Rangers bid millionaire Bill Miller enjoys high life with

[9] 27 April Statement on Rangers Football Club, www.ticketus.co.uk
[10] 'Bill Ng pulls out of race to buy stricken Rangers', *The Herald*, 20 April 2012

beauty queen lover'[11]. Revealing that Miller, who had divorced his wife in 2007, was now living with model and beauty pageant winner Becky Willard in his $2m beachside mansion, the article went on to wow us all with the revelation that 37-year-old Becky 'is poised to become the First Lady of Ibrox!'

As it happened, Becky's claim to the position of First Lady of Ibrox lasted only a matter of hours before boyfriend Bill pulled the plug on his bid and quickly followed Bill Ng into the mist. Whilst Miller's bid had attracted criticism from many quarters, and Rangers fans were wary of his proposals to liquidate the company, most fans were still prepared to give him a chance. But a tiny minority provided him with the escape clause he was doubtless looking for when they revealed their 'Yank go home!' banner at Rangers' last two home games of the season against St Mirren and Motherwell. Announcing that he had withdrawn his bid, Miller stated that he had received 'vitriolic' emails from fans, whilst casually noting that fresh information had come to light that revealed the seriousness of the club's finances.

Almost immediately, David Whitehouse, in one of his less ambiguous statements, announced that three other bidders had come forward to express their interest in buying the club and these offers were being 'evaluated with the utmost urgency'. It was at this stage that the name of Charles Green first came to light. Surprised and intrigued, we all wondered just who Green was, and who might comprise his mystery consortium. We also discovered that Bill Ng had re-entered the race for Rangers, clearly scenting an opportunity for a bargain, having allegedly been advised by Duff & Phelps that they were willing to accept 50 per cent of what he had initially offered. True to form, however, Ng's bid proved to be elusive and the self-professed 'lifelong Rangers fan' exited the stage, this time for good.

Meanwhile, tempers became frayed and the air waves filled with acri-monious charge and counter-charge as Brian Kennedy fulminated, during a televised press conference on 11 May, that Duff & Phelps would have 'blood on their hands' if they made another wrong call in picking the next preferred bidder. His statement came just hours after a last minute joint bid with Paul Murray and the Blue Knights was withdrawn.

Murray waded into the controversy claiming time had run out and

---

[11] Mark McGivern, 'Rangers bid millionaire Bill Miller enjoys high life with beauty queen lover', *Daily Record*, 5 May 2012

there was now 'a very real crisis'. He said Paul Clark had told him his offer of £8.5m would be enough to swing the deal if Craig Whyte's shares could be secured. Kennedy claimed that Duff & Phelps had advised that their bid was 'looking quite good' because the other parties were 'way behind'. Duff & Phelps, however, immediately retaliated by accusing Kennedy and Murray of putting together a package that was 'no better than liquidation', claiming that their funding model was based 'on fanciful dreams of future European conquests'. Whatever the truth, Brian Kennedy and Paul Murray had failed in their bid to take control of Rangers. Perplexed and at their wits end, Rangers supporters watched and listened with mounting anxiety as the bidding saga descended into farce.

Meanwhile, the *Daily Record* had not been idle and immediately published allegations that new bidder Charles Green had previously had business dealings with a finance firm connected to Craig Whyte. The paper also described him as having had 'a chequered commercial past'. Other reports asserted that he had been forced out of his job as chief executive at Sheffield United by fans after selling their best players, whilst *Sportsmail* reported that 'a senior figure from Green's time at Bramall Lane' was warning fans that he should not be allowed anywhere near Rangers Football Club. The same paper reported an un-named source as saying:

> He [Charles Green] is not what Rangers want or need. If he's backed by the same sort of people who were behind him at United, it's bye bye Rangers.[12]

Just a few days later, however, Charles Green and his consortium agreed a deal, reportedly worth £8.5m, to take over Rangers, and were speedily named as the preferred bidder by Duff & Phelps. Charles Green enthused:

> This is a great football club with a tremendous history and we will preserve that while building a solid platform for the future. Rangers supporters have every right to believe their club should be a success on and off the pitch and that is exactly what we will strive to achieve.[13]

Rangers fans remained sceptical and internet blogs were full of speculation about Green's consortium: who were they and did they have the

---

[12] John Greechan, 'Blood on their hands! Kennedy savages the Rangers administrators', *The Daily Mail*, 11 May 2012

[13] Statement announcing Charles Green as new owner of Rangers, STV website, news.stv.tv/scotland/99547-in-full-statement-announcing-charles-green-as-new-owner-of-rangers/, 13 May 2012

required financial clout to run Rangers Football Club? But working in the background, shunning publicity and diligently building a sustainable bid in private, well beyond the intrusion of the media, Charles Green had pulled together his consortium in such a persuasive manner that Duff & Phelps were prepared to offer him exclusivity.

The fans knew little of Green and were rightly cautious. They had been misled by Craig Whyte, and were determined that it would not be allowed to happen again. Opposition to Green's bid began to build and was fuelled by his inability to disclose details of the members of his consortium. The internet was hot with speculation, and bloggers were busily trying to track down whatever information they could on the few names that had been linked to Green in press reports – names such as, Arif Masood Naqvi, Imran Ahmad, Alessandro Celano, and the mysterious and intriguing Blue Pitch Holdings. Who were they, and why did they want to buy our club? Charles Green was under the microscope – and under fire.

In an article written for *Rangers Media* around this time, I argued that, in the current atmosphere of uncertainty and heightened tensions surrounding the future of our club, there was a real danger that we would rush to unfair and unsubstantiated conclusions. I also argued there was no evidence to suggest he was anything other than a legitimate and honest businessman and fans should not be unduly influenced by media innuendo and unfounded allegations. Nothing the press had said about Green had demonstrated any wrongdoing, improper conduct or dishonesty on his part, and I pointed out that there was a very real danger he would be condemned before we had an opportunity to assess him and, more importantly, his consortium's bid for the club.

In a swift, incisive and no-nonsense response that would quickly become his hallmark, Green answered his detractors, and particularly those Rangers fans who doggedly continued to promote the now defunct Blue Knights. He declared:

> Without us this club would have closed. When I get these comments that the Blue Knights consortium was going to do this or that I say 'Get your cheques out and buy it!'[14]

In the months to come, fans would become accustomed to Green's often

---

[14] Roddy Forsyth, 'Charles Green: Rangers fans can trust my takeover', *The Telegraph*, 10 June 2012

blunt and outspoken manner, but would also very quickly come to respect his forthright defence of the club. Under fire he may have been, but he had fired a telling shot. As Charles Green completed his £5.5m acquisition of Rangers Football Club on 14 June 2012, he was unaware of the scandals that would unfold during July as the SFA/SPL exerted yet more pressure on Rangers.

Thankfully, the traumas of 2012 are slowly being consigned to the past. The continued, awe-inspiring support and commitment of Rangers fans around the world, phenomenal season ticket sales and a hugely successful share issue have seen the club slowly regain its strength and confidence. In his book, *A Complete History of Scotland's Greatest Football Club*, John Fairgrieve said:

> And always, in this broad picture of Scottish football, one name towers above the rest like a colossus, and the name is, of course, Rangers. There is no getting away from it, nor is there any reason one should try and get away from it. The club, the fans, the players all have their imperfections, but Rangers are the greatest club in Scotland, have been so for many years, and probably always will be, as long as the game is played. This is a fact of football life, and cannot reasonably be argued with.[15]

We recently celebrated our 140th anniversary and can now look forward with some confidence to another 140 years. I will not be around to see them, but my grandchildren and their children and grandchildren will. To those who have shamed Scottish football with their attempts to denigrate our club, I say simply that you have wasted your time, because our club will never die.

---

[15] John Fairgrieve, *The Rangers: A Complete History of Scotland's Greatest Football Club*, (Hale, 1964)

CHAPTER III

Social Media and the Rangers Ownership Battle

W STEWART FRANKLIN

THE LAST TWO years have been genuinely historic times for Rangers Football Club – albeit perhaps not in the kind of positive terms as other significant periods in the 141 year timeline of the club.

From the initial sale of the club to Craig Whyte in 2011, right through to the Charles Green-led consortium's purchase, it has been a roller-coaster ride for Rangers fans. Add in the raw, but always developing, effect of social media and online media coverage generally, and this has been a truly unique situation for Scottish news and sport.

As the owner of a popular independent fans website which has been part of the online Rangers community for over ten years, it's this development of internet debate which has interested me most – more so when examined closely in the context of what has happened at our club. It seems that online discussion forums have gone from extremist domains of 'keyboard cowboys'[1] to busy networks of potential customers frequented by the clubs themselves: be it official club Facebook pages with hundreds of thousands of 'followers', right through to the captain of Rangers and the manager of Celtic taking an active part in Twitter debates. That's a remarkable credibility transformation by anyone's standards.

Of course websites and social media are strange beasts. Libertarians everywhere proclaim them as the bastions of free speech and the catalysts to people power while the Scottish Government passes expensive new laws to police 'threatening communications'.[2] On any one day – or indeed, in any one thread of debate – one can see both arguments: the consumer arguing his case with the multi-national; the voter highlighting issues

---

[1] Keith Jackson, 'Gordon Strachan: Keyboard cowboys have hijacked Scottish football', *Daily Record*, 16 February 2011

[2] Amy Goulding and Ben Cavanagh, *Religiously Aggravated Offending in Scotland 2011–12*, Scottish Government Social Research 2012, www.scotland. gov.uk/Resource/0040/00408745.pdf, 23 November 2012

with his local MP; or, sadly, the bigot abusing the innocent sports star or celebrity. Separating the wheat from the chaff has never been so time consuming or as expensive to the taxpayer.

With this in mind, the battle for the ownership of Rangers wasn't just going to happen in boardrooms or courts but in the online propaganda war (for that's what it was) between those trying to kill the club, those trying to save it and those looking to buy it. From the official club social networking pages (Rangers FC has around 300,000 Facebook 'likes' and just over 100,000 Twitter 'followers') publicising the latest information to an award winning (though still anonymous and now discredited) anti-Rangers tax blog, events were carried out in the public eye to the smallest minutiae.

To that end, in this chapter I will speak with the club's social media officer on how he thinks his field has developed over the last two years. I'll also ask two respected journalists how the mainstream media viewed the role of previously distrusted website contributors in conjunction with welcoming them onto their pages and programmes to form the narrative. Finally, I'll detail my own unusual part in one foreign bidder's attempt to buy the club.

Interview with Robert Boyle
(Social Media Officer – Rangers Football Club)

On their official website, Rangers FC detail the main reasons for joining social networks as the club 'being open to all' and 'being proud' of their 'football family'. Initially the club joined Facebook and Twitter in the summer of 2011 but have since added a presence on Flickr, Soundcloud and Storify. Full details of all their social networks can be found on the club's website but we also found out more from Robert Boyle who has spent the last 18 months building the club's online profile.

Q *What inspired Rangers to come up with a social networking campaign?*

A Rangers were relatively late starters in terms of social media and the road to an official presence on the different platforms started long before my time with the club.

There are always potential pitfalls for any business launching a social media presence and for Rangers those were perhaps only magnified with different challenges that are unique to the club. However, the club realised that the opportunities outweighed any potential risks and that steps could be taken to mitigate any potential problems.

The club realised there were existing communities on different social media platforms and that it was in our best interests to be part of those conversations and, where possible, leading them.

When I joined the club in May 2011, we started by launching a Facebook page with considerable success. Once we had an official presence there, we quickly moved onto the other platform identified as having a considerable Rangers community, Twitter.

I feel the club is now very much part of the online Rangers communities on these platforms and the others that we have since launched. It's my belief that fans are appreciating the accessibility, openness and closeness between the club and the fan base that social media can facilitate. This is something we will strive to continue to build on this season and beyond.

Q *What would you consider the biggest successes of your time at the club?*

A There is no doubt the travails faced by the supporters of Rangers in the last 12 months have played a significant part in awakening a unity and togetherness within our supporter base.

In my opinion, social media has been the medium where fans have found a common voice and a forum to discuss everything associated with the club on top of being the place where fans source their day to day news. It's not an outlandish statement to make now that social media for many is the first thing they check in the morning and the last thing they check at night.

The strategy we have in place for social media means that fans can get closer to their club than ever before, be it by seeing exclusive behind the scenes content, the latest news straight from the club or following what's happening in live matches wherever they are in the world.

Something that I felt was important was adding a personal touch for supporters – something that helps to build the sense of togetherness and having club staff with different skillsets on social media was important.

Now fans can, for the first time in my opinion, ask questions directly of the club if they have any problems or queries and get a response from a person representing the club in a medium where they also talk to their friends.

The number of users following key platforms, Facebook and Twitter, has continued to grow month on month. However, I don't personally feel raw numbers are a good yardstick of how we are performing because it's much more prudent to analyse the levels of engagement by our fans. It is in these key indicators that we are having great success and continuing to innovate and improve.

Q *What improvements can be made and how do you see the social field developing?*

A I think there is a real chance for the relationship between the club and our fans to continue to be strengthened through social media and the digital world in general.

As technology continues to evolve and improve it will become ever easier for fans to get their daily fix of all things Rangers. Whilst these improvements will mean the fan can get closer than ever to the club they love, they will also continue to make it easier for the club to understand exactly what fans want.

Supporter sentiment analysis is important to us and the conversational nature of a platform such as Twitter means that ideas and plans can easily be bounced off fans of different ages and situations in a manner that isn't stuffy or corporate. It's never been easier to ask our fans openly what it is that they like and what they don't like.

The club recognises how important its supporters are moving forward and the club is ready to embrace fully the continued evolution of digital and social media and realise the great opportunity afforded through these platforms to strengthen the essential bond between the club and its fans.

Interview with Peter Smith (Scottish Television) and Richard Wilson (The Herald)

One doesn't have to go far to see the image of online football supporters mocked. Whether it is the new Scotland international team manager Gordon Strachan suggesting internet users 'are people who have no friends' or even Rangers' new Director of Communications James Traynor describing anonymous bloggers as 'supporters with dangerous agendas hidden under the banner of integrity'[3], it's never a surprise to see often unfair generalisations bandied about by people who don't even take part in online discussions.

---

[3] James Traynor, 'Why this is my last ever newspaper column', *Daily Record*, 3 December 2012

Of course what these people don't mention is the huge popularity of such websites and their own employers' often indecent haste in wanting to engage with them. After all, the Scottish Football Association has its own Twitter account while the *Daily Record* has busy comments facilities for those who wish to discuss the latest event or story in the newspaper. Add in regular media appearances from the previously unknown bloggers on TV, radio and in print, then it's difficult to ignore the effect of the internet age on the erstwhile more recognised forms of media.

Two journalists who do realise the importance of social networking are Peter Smith of STV's *Scotland Tonight* and Richard Wilson of *The Herald* – both of whom regularly used Twitter to engage with supporters of all football clubs as the Rangers story developed in 2012.

Q *At what point did you make the conscious decision to get involved in social networking? Was it a personal choice or suggested by your employer?*

RICHARD WILSON: I opened my Twitter account when I left *The Sunday Times* and spent four months as a freelance. I recognised the importance for journalists in this digital media age of raising your profile, but also as a way to promote your work, try to bring it to new audiences and, frankly, to people who may potentially offer new commissions. At the time, I didn't use it much, but after moving to *The Herald*, I found it particularly helpful during the 2010 World Cup. I was writing analysis pieces about aspects of the tournament, and following journalists who were in South Africa kept me up to date with all the pieces they were filing. Since then, I used it regularly, opening that use out to include interacting with people who take the time to make a comment – positive or negative – about something I've written. Mostly, it's good fun, you always learn something new, and it's become an invaluable resource.

PETER SMITH: Twitter came to my attention in 2010. I was already aware it was beginning to rise above other online communications tools and more and more people were talking about interacting with TV programmes and celebrities with this new medium. I decided to try it out as a personal choice, despite having little clue as to how it worked or why it was of any use to me.

My initial impression was it felt a little like talking to an empty room – I would tweet but there wouldn't always be a reply. Gaining followers in niche subjects was key, and I decided to focus on politics and current affairs for work, and my passion – football – for fun.

Joining in with relevant discussions and offering good content is also what makes you worth following, and I have learned to stick to subjects in which I am confident my contribution is worth sharing.

Q *What advantages and disadvantages are there in such an involvement?*

RW The advantages are that you and your work reach a wider audience, but also that the audience can reach you. It breaks down the boundaries between writer and reader. Your timeline often becomes a resource though, such as breaking stories and good feature/analysis pieces while providing a depth and range of coverage that the traditional media cannot manage (European football, MLS, etc.). The only disadvantages are that you can spend an inordinate amount of time on Twitter, and occasionally you receive the odd abusive message, but they're only minor issues.

PS I quickly realised that the strength of Twitter, from a journalist's perspective, is not in sending out your own thoughts; it's in following the right people. We can now connect with genuine experts who can give regular updates as well as offer answers to questions almost instantly.

These days, before I turn on the TV or radio in the morning, I check Twitter for news updates. I find out what's trending and what my favourite tweeters are talking about. In that regard, Twitter has broken new ground as an alternative 'wires' service which brings breaking news, comment and analysis. This kind of instant feedback has changed news forever and it has now become an established and integral part of my job.

The disadvantages all stem from the lack of accountability. People can spread incorrect information and it often gets repeated incredibly quickly and widely. It can get mixed with elements of truth and become accepted as fact without people questioning the credibility of the source. Journalists are trained from an early stage to verify everything: check the sources and get something on the record yourself. Not everyone in media adheres to this but it's the standard for making sure you're not simply repeating someone else's mistakes. For example, when using Twitter as a source of news we must remember it is not coming through a credible medium like the Press Association or Reuters. It is unverified and tweets should always be treated as a potential lead rather than a solid source.

And then there's the bombardment of abuse which comes your way, particularly when tweeting about Scottish football, but that's part of the terrain here. Anyone who's grown up in the West of Scotland understands this, and we know the boundaries of acceptability. As long as it doesn't go beyond those boundaries, it doesn't bother me.

Q   *How crucial was it to actively seek the opinion of Rangers supporters online during the takeover process and how did this affect your own outlook?*

RW It was crucial to stay on top of the mood of the Rangers support, because it was an active participant in the takeover process. The Rangers Supporters Trust (RST) were trying to push ahead with their plans to buy a stake in the club, but the response of supporters to the various interested parties had an impact on the takeover process. Twitter was one important tool for this. In terms of outlook, it informed how I represented the Rangers support in pieces.

PS Twitter is excellent for crowd-sourcing. That includes seeking opinion and testing the waters of public mood for important subjects. I regularly ask for people's views on subjects because Twitter is at its best when used as a two-way medium. Particularly with a story as big as that which affected Rangers in 2012 it was vital not to make assumptions. Events changed so quickly, I had to keep checking how fans were reacting to developments to fully understand the impact. Twitter also provides an easy way to engage with the many Rangers supporters who were demanding, rightly, to have their voice heard on something that ultimately affected them more than anyone.

Q   *With so many relevant people previously criticising the contribution of online football fans, was it not a concern to include them in your articles or programmes?*

RW That depends how you include them. Twitter allowed an introduction to confident, thoughtful, strong-minded Rangers fans, and they could often be approached to articulate the fans' point of view. In terms of sources, I held conversations with several people, privately, that I also interacted with on Twitter, but as a journalist I would never have taken information at face value, at least until I built up a better understanding of the person as a source, and the credibility of their information. Twitter is a useful tool, so long as you use it properly. It's the same as a person phoning me with some information. How I react to that information depends on how well I know the person, trust them, know where it has come from, etc.

PS Twitter can sometimes be a mix of salient points and incoherent anger being vented. Too often the most persistent voices are heard before the more sensible ones, and this can warp the discourse of a discussion. I also try to remember there can be a poignant disparity between the views of the online community of football fans and those supporters I know who regularly attend matches but never use Twitter or internet forums. Online comments should not be treated as the definitive opinion of real fans. Perhaps that's one of the most important lessons Scottish football has learned in 2012.

Q   *The Rangers Tax Case (RTC) site is arguably the primary example of how an anonymous blog can direct the narrative of a story. How would you describe its contribution and that of similar websites?*

RW   At first, RTC was a source of detailed and significant information. However, the site quickly became a forum for anti-Rangers discussions, and the author of the blog was quite clear about their own allegiance. Remaining anonymous also presented a problem. As a journalist, you had to ask yourself if you could take the information seriously given the clear bias of the author, and indeed the commentators on the blog, while the anonymity meant that you could not verify anything with them. It also became clear that the information was limited, although very detailed. The author took what we had to presume as an informed stance on what their information meant. As it turned out, the information was correct – and clearly leaked from somewhere – but the analysis turned out to be wrong. The contribution was important, though, because RTC, and other active Celtic-minded bloggers, helped to generate the hysteria of the 'Rangers are cheats' narrative that prevailed last summer. At the time, nobody could be certain about the outcome of the First Tier Tax Tribunal, but a loud and persistent group of people on social media pushed a certain point of view that became mainstream opinion. They turned out to be wrong.

PS   I have great respect for anyone who made a contribution to the Rangers story because it was a complex and dynamic series of events which confounded most of us at one time or another. That's why people looked for experts to put their faith in. The RTC site clearly had access to exclusive information which carried a great deal of weight, and it captured the interest of fans and journalists alike. Sadly, its contributors used their privileged position of having unique access to information on the Rangers tax case to attack Scottish journalists, for some reason, as though it was the media's fault for not having

access to the RTC source. Their contributors also attempted to dictate the narrative of the story in such a way that it was easy for fans
to believe the tax case was a foregone conclusion.

I had a few Twitter altercations with the RTC people in which I
was accused of all sorts because I stuck to my journalistic principles
of telling people not to assume guilt until a verdict was delivered.
Perhaps the most surprising aspect of it, for me, was the willingness
with which people accepted everything an anonymous blogger told
them. It reflects the low levels of trust between football fans in Scotland
and the journalists, but it's concerning because, unlike the people
behind RTC, journalists operate in the open and in an industry which
still, for the most part, works to important standards of truth. Ultimately, people would have been better served by following the fundamental standards of awaiting a verdict before presuming anything.

Q *Do you think the ownership story would have unfolded differently
without the internet effect? For example, would matters have happened so quickly or would we still be talking about Craig Whyte as
the Rangers owner?*

RW Craig Whyte's regime was only ever going to be short, because he
did not have the funds to run Rangers and was arguably systemati-
cally destroying the club from within. Traditional media were also
among the main sources of stories about the way he was running the
club – along with an important and significant contribution from
social media. I'm not sure the ownership saga would have worked
out differently, since ultimately it was about money and negotiating
the best deal, but the internet had the effect of maintaining the
intensity and scrutiny on those involved.

PS I have no idea how it would have changed. Rangers' problems which
resulted in the liquidation of the OldCo run much deeper than a
battle being fought with dedicated haters on the internet. People are
accountable for what happened and must be challenged widely. They
should not be able to rely on the loyalty of the Rangers fans for providing them with something of a shield.

I also think football fans in general will always have a great deal
of difficulty in accepting impartial criticism of the people employed
by the club they love. Rangers fans remain vigilant because of what's
happened at Ibrox – and perhaps with very good reason – but many
of them are still too guarded when it comes to healthy criticism from
journalists.

Q *How do you see the effect of social networks developing over the coming years?*

RW It will only increase. During the Rangers saga, it became clear to me that keeping stories quiet for the following day's paper was increasingly difficult, and at times impossible. Twitter was very much a part of that, because it was a fast-moving story and plenty of people were tapped into it, so few news lines held. Yet, despite that, newspaper sales increased, as we provided analysis, insight, context and perspective, as well as continuing to break stories. There was, and still is to an extent, a 'them and us' attitude between new and old media, but the Rangers story went a long way to dismantling that. Coverage would be poorer if it was one or the other. Clubs themselves can also communicate directly with their fans through social media, so I believe we will all be using these tools to a far greater extent in the coming years.

PS I hope it leads to more transparency, more accountability, and a greater level of understanding among people. Sadly, it sometimes feels like a playground for strangers to come together and argue. But it has great potential and we shouldn't discount how it is already bringing people together into open discussions. It should help journalists and news consumers, and we should use it to break down divisions rather than create conflict.

Interview with a source close to the UK representatives of Bill Ng (*Singaporean bidder for Rangers* FC)

As someone who has been involved in the online Rangers community for over ten years, it's fascinating how being a website owner can affect your life. Running an unofficial site for such a long period of time certainly has its ups and downs. Clearly, there is a lot of unnoticed time and effort which goes into maintaining websites – not to mention the associated financial costs and legal risks. On the other hand, an increased personal profile can be a positive in terms of working constructively with your peers in the support and obtaining the odd snippet of 'inside info' from people you meet along the way. Even if such information is not always accurate!

It was with that necessary qualification in mind that I approached a unique situation that faced me last spring at the height of the Rangers ownership battle. Although eventual Rangers owner Charles Green had not yet showed his hand, there were still a few parties genuinely interested in buying the club from Craig Whyte. In the UK corner we had the 'Blue Knights' – a team of high net-worth Rangers supporting businessmen; in the American corner we had Bill Miller – a transport tycoon from Tennessee; and, finally we had a consortium of wealthy Asian businessmen led by Bill Ng from Singapore. Thus, it's safe to say there was worldwide interest in the Rangers story.

During this period I had developed a few contacts in relevant areas and although it was still difficult to separate fact from fiction, I was often able to report accurate material on the rapidly changing ownership story. Indeed, it was often a race between my site (and other unofficial sites) and the mainstream media to be the first with exclusive news – so much so that the media were coming to me requesting more detail and slots on TV and radio. I appeared on *Sky Sports News* and was quoted in *The Straits Times* of Singapore which demonstrated the global media were interested in ordinary fan opinion.

This came to a head in early April 2012 when I conducted a live Q&A session on Twitter with Bill Ng's UK representatives discussing their negotiations to buy Rangers. To my knowledge this hadn't happened before online and certainly hasn't happened since. Why then, did Ng and his UK team consider the social media influence so important?

Q   *This time last year must have been a fascinating period in your business career. How did you become involved in the Rangers ownership battle?*

A   I was in Singapore on business on 14 February, having dinner with Bill, when news came through of the club going into administration. It immediately became the only conversation around the table and Bill expressed a strong interest in going after Rangers. We felt the bid could be funded in the Far East but controlled in Glasgow. We made contact with Duff & Phelps expressing interest and I flew back to Glasgow where I pulled together a team of businessmen, all experts in their fields (and all 'Bluenoses'), who would have run the club. We appointed professional advisers to steer us through the process.

Q   *As I quickly found out myself, the situation was one that often changed on an hourly basis. How did you stay up-to-date with events?*

A   We conducted a constant media monitor of broadcast, newspaper and social media channels. This allowed us to keep on top of issues as they developed, and react accordingly. That proved valuable, as we were trying to remain anonymous. Members of the team were able to use contacts in football, the media and business to build a better picture of developments.

Q   *Obviously, you and Bill must have felt unofficial media channels were vital in a PR sense. Why did you decide to use an independent website to communicate with Rangers fans?*

A   The Rangers story will go down in history as a case study on how social media drove events and shaped outcomes. Views were being expressed on all sides and comment was being made about Bill and our bid, often inaccurate and sometimes malicious. Anyone involved in an acquisition ideally wants to stay in the background until a deal is completed but that was proving impossible. We wanted to put our case directly to Rangers supporters and we needed a credible outlet, read and respected by fans and run by intelligent people offering balanced views. That's why we chose *Gersnet*.

Q   *At the time, most fans appreciated the direct route but, looking back, do you think such an engagement hindered your efforts to be seen as a credible buyer for the club?*

A   No – not at all. Newspapers and broadcasters express their own views editorially, despite your best efforts to paint the clearest picture. We were very comfortable communicating and talking to supporters through *Gersnet* – an independent and respected website. We appreciated the platform we were being given to outline to fans that Bill's bid was genuine and credible and how we intended to move the club forward with our plans for Rangers.

Q   *Which parts of trying to buy the club did you enjoy most? And was there anything that proved frustrating?*

A   The interest in Rangers was amazing. We were prepared for that but it took over my life. It was exhausting but very exciting. The situation was very confused and complex and discussions with the Administrators were demanding, with so many problems to confront and overcome. My big regret is that the team didn't get the chance to turn around Rangers and put in place the plans we had for the club.

Q   *Did you invest in the recent Initial Public Offering and do you see yourself or Bill Ng involved in the club in the future?*

A   No, I didn't. Bill is a fan and keeps a close eye on how everything is developing at Ibrox. He still feels the revenue potential he recognised in the Far East and Asia is there to be exploited for the benefit of

Rangers. His research showed Rangers are recognised as one of the leading British clubs among fans in those regions. Who knows what the future holds?

In a general sense, there's no doubt the way football supporters consume their information has changed markedly since the onset of the digital age. No longer do fans have to wait until the next day to find out the latest news (or indeed watch the latest match) but the 24/7 nature of the internet and especially social media means debate is instant and can be easily influenced.

In that respect, it seems obvious from our contributors that online football supporters (and specifically those that use social media) were utilised in a range of different ways during the Rangers takeover process. Not only did more orthodox forms of the Fourth Estate monitor a variety of site and individual blog opinion to help form their coverage, it's clear from Bill Ng's UK representatives that it was vital for them to reach as many fans as possible by conducting a unique Q&A via Twitter. 'Tomorrow's news today' has never been more apt.

On the other hand, it's less easy to define the part social media played in the ownership battle *per se*. While we can't deny its imprint in some areas, I don't think we can say with any great confidence sites like Twitter and Facebook directly affected the sale or the overall process. Ultimately Craig Whyte's mismanagement, Administrators Duff & Phelps and the emergence of Charles Green decided that particular story. Nevertheless, the part the internet played in terms of the general Rangers narrative over the past two years should not be under-estimated. Bill Ng's team certainly feel the social aspect may form part of the strategy for similar deals in the future.

With this in mind, Rangers were among the first to invest in their social media activities and many other Scottish clubs have followed since. The numbers involved and the successes highlighted by Robert Boyle show just how important it is to have an 'official' voice taking an active part in such forums. Indeed, this engagement will only increase as the way clubs (and football leagues) deliver their media evolves over time. From the more simple days of *Scotsport* on TV at Sunday tea-time, to Rangers TV and YouTube on our smartphones at any time and in any place, the consumer is no longer limited to their front room. Furthermore, while in the past clubs may have argued over gate receipt splits, falling match-day crowds means media rights are now just as much (if not more) a bone of contention.

In a similar vein, sales of more traditional forms of media such as print newspapers are declining so it's no surprise to see newspapers and their journalists making the leap to more modern technology. In March 2013, while much of Europe remained in the grip of austerity and recession, it was interesting to note the British Retail Consortium (BRC) reported 'sales in February were up 2.7 per cent on the previous year' which was led by sales of electrical goods 'including tablets and computers'[4]. Thus, as noted previously, the effects of social media will only increase as more and more people access their information using online methods.

With regard to Rangers, our social media numbers may be impressive at first glance but, as with most media exposure, we have some way to go before we can match the 'bigger' clubs. For example, Barcelona has over 8m Twitter followers while Arsenal (the most followed UK team) has over 2m[5]. Obviously these numbers may not be indicative of actual club supporters but they do reflect online media interest in football worldwide and that may help empirically explain why Charles Green was able to attract IPO investment as far away as Asia. It's often argued that we now live in a global village so every business is under pressure to make the most of such an opportunity.

In conclusion, Rangers Football Club is not a club (or company) that is sold very often. Before the unusual events of the past two years, Rangers have only arguably had two majority shareholders who could be considered beneficial owners: The Lawrence Group (run by John Lawrence then his grandson Lawrence Marlborough) from 1963 until 1988 when David Murray bought the club through his company.[6] It's doubtful any of these historic figures had much media coverage to deal with as they got involved with the club over the course of the 20th century. Although, as we saw when Murray International Holdings tried to sell, the internet age was starting to have a real effect on the disposing of a business.

After Charles Green's recent resignation, the current controlling interest at Rangers may or may not last as long as previous ownerships but I think it's safe to say those who own our club have unprecedented media coverage to deal with. The social media phenomenon is something we may all just be getting to grips with but there seems little doubt it will be a necessary and much valued commodity going forward.

---

4   Sky News, 'Retail Sales Driven Up By Tablet Demand', news.sky.com/story/ 1060201/retail-sales-driven-up-by-tablet-demand, 5 March 2013

5   folos.im, 'League Table of Twitter Followers'

6   Keith Sinclair, 'Builder who laid foundations of Ibrox revolution. Lawrence dynasty grew from humble beginnings to sow seeds of Rangers' success', *The Glasgow Herald*, 8 February 1997

CHAPTER IV

Where are all the Rangers Men?

COLIN ARMSTRONG

THE EVENTS OF 2012 – and the subsequent aftershocks – have undoubt-edly left a deep scar on every Rangers supporter. To watch the club so viciously attacked from all quarters has left a lot of ill feeling among the supporters, some of which may never completely go away. But that, for me, was not the main issue with the financial meltdown that occurred at Ibrox.

Managing expectations and redrawing boundaries was a difficult, but necessary, process on being presented with the news that the SPL had said 'No to NewCo' and trap-doored the club to the bottom tier of Scottish football. This was not going to be the successful Rangers that I had grown up with. In terms of quality, this wasn't even going to be the Rangers I had endured in the early- to mid-1980s, prior to Graeme Souness arriving and reinstalling some pride and presence around a club that had been on the wane since a certain sunny day in Lisbon in 1967.

The Rangers sides of the early 1980s would prove to be a good barometer for attending Ibrox in this new age as you certainly managed expectations with Bobby Williamson as your striker. But despite the mediocrity, I still look back on that period with fondness. Maybe it was because it was the era when I really started supporting Rangers, or maybe it's because times seemed that bit simpler. Whatever the reason, I still get goosebumps when I see that pinstriped shirt or when I see a YouTube clip of Rangers from that period. The likes of Cooper, Russell, John MacDonald and Peter McCloy still have a capacity to stir something deep inside me. These were normal, working class guys playing for the club most of them supported as boys. They were paid more than the average man on the street, but they weren't earning in a week what most of us earn in a year. And because of that, I loved them. They felt like they were mine.

Those who are old enough to remember Souness signing from Samp-doria have drawn comparisons between his arrival and Rangers starting a new chapter in the bottom tier. I can certainly say that the early stages of this season had a similar buzz and purpose to the days when Souness, Butcher and the rest strode up Edmiston Drive. The one difference, however, was the players – and I don't just mean in terms of their ability and quality.

The arrival of Souness was the catalyst for a string of players eloping north of the border to ply their trade in Govan. The traditional movement had been the other way; Scottish players heading south for the relative riches of the English First Division. The horror of 39 fans dying in the Heysel Stadium disaster in 1985 meant English clubs were enduring a five year ban from European football and Souness saw an opportunity to bring the cream of the crop to Ibrox. The Great Ship Souness was about to set sail, and everyone who was anyone wanted on board – even if they weren't from a traditional Rangers background. Compare that to 2012 – when Whyte steered the club into an iceberg, and the men we deemed heroes with traditional Rangers backgrounds were looking for the quickest way off the sinking ship – and it is obvious that any similarities between these two periods end there.

This was the realisation supporters found most difficult to deal with: playing for Rangers no longer meant what it once did. To watch those who once represented the club, and kissed the badge whilst doing so, look for the most profitable exit left a feeling of betrayal that will not be forgotten any time soon. That some who committed these acts of greed portrayed themselves as 'Rangers men' merely poured salt into a gaping wound.

To be a Rangers supporter is to be brought up on a wealth of players who fall into the 'he played for the jersey' bracket; men's men who not only guided the club to great glory on the field, but who protected its honour and integrity with their conduct off it. They considered themselves privileged to play for the club and were grief stricken when their time at Ibrox came to an end.

The arrival of Sky TV enhanced the wealth and professionalism of the game and took it to levels that could only have been dreamt of a few years previously. Suddenly clubs had dieticians, sports scientists and all manner of revenue streams to supplement them. Players had lawyers and agents to look after their every want and need. No longer would a player simply be someone who played for the club. He would be a commodity – a rather valuable one at that – and he would be paid the market rate in salary terms. The gap between the fan and the footballer has widened at an alarming rate over the last 20 years and never was that more exposed than in what happened at Rangers.

The announcement that Rangers had entered administration sent the supporters into a state of shock, panic and concern for what lay ahead for the club. There was also a fear for the staff. After all, this wasn't just a club to these people – it was their livelihoods. The players had security in the knowledge that their wares would be desired elsewhere if the worst came to the worst. The staff had no such safety net.

There followed a series of meetings between the players and Duff & Phelps in order to negotiate wage cuts. The possibility of some of them being made redundant also loomed large. Players such as Lee McCulloch, at the wrong side of 30 and on a decent wage, were deemed most at risk. Despite days of negotiating, there seemed to be no end to the uncertainty, with no real news coming from Ibrox in terms of agreeing wage cuts or redundancies. That lasted until 9 March when Duff & Phelps announced that Steven Whittaker, Steven Naismith and Steven Davis had agreed to a 75 per cent pay cut. It was reported that the three players had agreed the cut in order to avoid substantial job losses at the club. There was a hint of what was to come, however, in the words of Joint Administrator Paul Clark. He revealed that the delay in any announcement was due to a failure to agree certain clauses with players, but tried to defuse any thoughts they were negotiating an easier and cheaper way out of Ibrox during the summer:

> We will vary certain contracts such that there will be trigger points at which they can move. I don't think that should be considered that any or all of the players are considering that they want to leave the club in the summer. It's just a safety mechanism from their point of view, in exchange for the very substantial amounts they're giving up, to give them some flexibility depending on what the new ownership structure looks like when the club comes out of administration.

The priorities of supporters and players were now at completely different ends of the spectrum. The fans were out buying tickets and selling-out Ibrox for the remaining home games of the season. They were raising funds to aid the club and generally doing all they could to help it. Some players, it appeared, were intent on making sure they didn't lose out financially and seemed more worried about their own interests.

Despite this, it was a united front on match-days for the rest of the season. The supporters and the club joined together in unison for the remaining fixtures, the highlight of which was preventing Celtic winning the title at Ibrox with a victory that was a far more convincing than the 3–2 score line suggested. The final fixture of the season was at McDiarmid Park in Perth against St Johnstone. A convincing 4–0 win was achieved and the players headed down the tunnel to applause and chants ringing in their ears after a mini lap of honour. Nobody knew if we'd ever see any of them in a Rangers jersey again, but none of us were prepared to be dealt the blow that was in the post and heading to Ibrox with a first-class stamp on it.

On 12 June, the news broke that HMRC had decided to reject the Company Voluntary Arrangement proposed by Charles Green's consortium, thus forcing a company established in 1899 into liquidation. It was a devastating blow for the supporters and everyone at the club. Nothing was certain now. The club's place in the top flight was in jeopardy and nobody really expected the top players to stay if that was lost. But the events that followed in the days after 12 June have left a very sour taste in the mouth of not only supporters, but many connected with the club.

The first to speak was Lee McCulloch when he announced that he intended to stay with Rangers. It was news that warmed the hearts of Rangers fans everywhere. He told the *Sunday Mail*:

> I am going nowhere. I am staying with Rangers. Whether we're in the SPL, the Third Division or anywhere in between – I will be with Rangers. Since I was a kid growing up in Motherwell, all I wanted to do was play for the club and there is no way I will walk away. It's the last thing I would do. Wearing the Rangers jersey is an important part of my life and I'd never forgive myself if I gave that up. I don't believe this is a time for quitting Rangers. That would be the easy thing to do. This is a time for sticking with the club. I want to be with Rangers. That's all that matters to me. It's my view that we are still Glasgow Rangers. The Newco doesn't change anything for me.

This was music to the ears of the supporters. A player coming out and saying they still wanted to play for the Light Blues – and that Rangers were still Rangers. The corporate identity may have been lost, but the club remained, and McCulloch displayed some of its spirit not only by staying but also by being seemingly determined to take a major part in restoring it.

The good news provided by McCulloch was offset a few days later when Steven Naismith and Steven Whittaker held a press conference to announce they were refusing to transfer their contracts under the TUPE (Transfer of Undertakings and Protection of Employment) legislation to the NewCo. The news was bad enough because it denied the club any potential transfer fee, one that could have gone to paying some of the football debt which might have helped restore relations between the club and some of its detractors. But how it was delivered, particularly by Naismith, was hard to take. In front of the assembled media, the player who claimed to be a 'Rangers man' stated:

> I have discussed this decision with my fiancée, my family and my advisors.

It has been an extremely difficult decision to make but I believe it is the right decision. As players we were put in a difficult position by the Administrators whereby we were asked to take a 75 per cent pay cut to contracts that we entered into in good faith. As players we collectively saw this as the only way to get Rangers Football Club out of administration by way of a CVA and thereby protect the staff jobs and the history of the club and give the creditors who had also entered into contracts with Rangers in good faith the best chance of being paid.

Both Steven [Whittaker] and I and our agent fought hard with Administrators during negotiations to insert clauses that offered protection to staff and players at the club. I am extremely proud of the actions we took but I am disappointed and angry that Rangers Football Club no longer exists in its original form.

I am proud that the result of the squad's decision to take a 75 per cent pay cut for three months was successful in our aim of protecting the players and staff at Ibrox and Murray Park's conditions that has resulted in the opportunity for each member of staff to TUPE over or not to the new entity keeping their original pay and conditions.

It was bad enough for Naismith to talk as if he were some trade unionist who had defeated Thatcher and led the miners to glory, but to state that, in his opinion, the club no longer existed was deemed by many to be an unforgivable betrayal by the player. Many fans viewed it as an opportunistic act by someone who had spent half his Rangers career on the treatment table with two serious knee injuries. The club and the supporters had stood by Naismith during his time on the sidelines and when he was displaying indifferent form, yet when the club needed support, the player took the first available flight out of the club to the riches of the Premiership and Everton. He would not be the last to leave supporters feeling abandoned.

Following Naismith and Whittaker out the door were the likes of Allan McGregor, Kyle Lafferty and Steven Davis; stalwarts of the Walter Smith side that had secured three successive titles. None of them transferred to the new company and only in the case of Davis was any financial compensation agreed. The club is still seeking fees where the other players are concerned. Even the younger players were in on the act, with the likes of John Fleck and Jamie Ness abandoning the club that had given them a platform to play professional football. There could be no disguising that this was a free-for-all. A once great sporting institution was being reduced to watching its players, some arguably not fit enough to lace the boots of the stars who had represented it in the past, hold it to ransom and walk away.

Not many supporters expected these players to hang about and play in the Third Division. It wasn't so much that they had left the club but how they had gone about it. Naismith and Whittaker, among others, seemed to have their lockers cleared out the minute it was announced that liquidation of the OldCo was unavoidable. The feeling of betrayal was tangible and it is hard to imagine a moment anytime soon when such players will be welcomed back at Ibrox in any capacity. As Naismith admitted in an interview just before Christmas 2012:

> To be honest, at this moment I wouldn't go back to Ibrox for a game. A lot of fans aren't happy with what went on but you never know in the future.

The players who left Rangers in the summer are merely the symptom of an underlying problem. They are simply pawns in a game that has lost much of its soul and integrity. A game where players such as Ashley Cole can nearly crash his car on hearing he's only been offered £80,000 a week, and where Ronaldo is reportedly sad because new tax laws in Spain means his take-home pay is a mere hundreds of thousands per week. The problems that have surrounded Rangers over the past year point to a wider issue within the game: players' wages. It was only a matter of time before a bigger club faced serious financial difficulties due to the demands of the modern day, top flight footballer. They are industries in their own right – with an annual turnover that some medium size businesses would be very happy with.

David Beckham, the Alpha Male of contemporary footballers, is a prime example. The poster boy of the modern game recently joined Paris Saint-Germain and announced immediately that he was giving away his salary to a local children's charity. Guys nodded their heads in appreciation of a proper geezer, ladies swooned at this act of generosity from a true gentleman and everyone found yet another reason to love Beckham, the thoroughly decent chap. What was not so widely recognised was the estimation that Beckham earned $255m over the five years he was in the US. Of that, only $32.5m was his baseline salary. The rest was made up of revenue sharing with his club LA Galaxy, endorsements, appearances and licensing. In short, Beckham gave away a relative pittance when he joined PSG, as his other interests would more than make up for any shortfall in his baseline salary.

Sandy Jardine is a Rangers veteran who made over 600 appearances between 1967 and 1982 and was a part of that famous team that secured the European Cup Winners' Cup in Barcelona in 1972. He is a legend in the eyes of supporters, and was not for mincing his words when asked about the players who had left the club. He said:

> I am dismayed and disappointed by the actions of the players. You have to say that if the players were up front and honest you would respect them more. What they have done is seen an opportunity, whether it is them or their agents, to maximise their income. The players took a salary sacrifice but for that they got clauses in their contracts which would allow them to leave on rock bottom prices if clubs came in for them. I have to be honest and I think the players have used our predicament to their gain.

There were not too many voices of protest at Jardine's stinging words. The fans felt the man who had represented Rangers admirably through a stellar career at Ibrox had hit the nail on the head. Greed and opportunism had ruled the day, and that hurt those who had once looked upon those players as heroes.

The level of feeling towards some ex-players was so strong that it gave those who decided to stay at the club, or move to it despite its now lowly placing, instant hero status. They were viewed as having stayed or come for the fight – to help Rangers get back to their rightful place in Scottish football. Despite this perception and the immense goodwill bestowed on them by grateful supporters, the reality has often been disappointing. Francisco Sandaza, for example, embarrassed the club, not to mention himself, when he was duped by a Celtic fan posing as an agent. In an act of naivety, Sandaza willingly disclosed his contract details, revealed that he only came to Rangers for the money and that he would move in a shot if a better deal became available. The perpetrator was recording the conversation and posted it online for the world to hear. Sandaza was immediately suspended and later sacked by the club following an internal investigation. It was no revelation to find out that the Spaniard had come to Ibrox for the money, but to hear him willingly tout himself behind the club's back exposed yet another footballer who was opportunistic to the point of dropping all basic levels of good due process – such as confirming that the stranger on the phone was indeed who he said he was. It appears that the prospect of earning more money in a warmer country temporarily suspended Sandaza's ability to practice the most basic of common sense.

Faced with players deserting the club, the Sandaza incident and accusations that the players haven't been focused or professional in their attempts to secure the Third Division title, it's hard not to come to the conclusion that being a Ranger doesn't carry the same prestige that it once did. That was the initial conclusion I came to during the past year – watching so many players walk out had made it difficult to think anything else. So when the club offered me the chance to speak to vice-captain Lee Wallace about his experience since coming to Rangers, I accepted, unsure whether he could offer me any evidence to change that view.

Sitting in the plush surroundings of the club's Auchenhowie training complex, I spoke at length with Wallace about his reasons for coming to, and staying with, Rangers. Wallace arrived from Hearts a few months before the club went into administration, and decided to stay on after Rangers were banished to the lower leagues. Why would a younger player with a potential international career want to play in the Third Division?

> It was a massive club with the chance of playing European football. At that point there were a lot of top players that were winners; they had a vast experience of winning trophies year after year.
>
> Rangers were the top team in my eyes at that point. There were a couple of bids and eventually when the third one was accepted, I was through the next day. We actually played Hearts that weekend, so I had trained more with Hearts that week than I had with Rangers which was a bit tough mentally. But to play with Rangers, a massive club, and play in front of 50,000 every second week was a big attraction.

That Wallace chose to stay on, despite one of the main reasons for signing – European football – being lost for the foreseeable future, makes his loyalty to the club even more commendable. And you are left wondering if he ever considered leaving Rangers like so many others:

> Obviously there was a lot of thinking time over the summer, but it never really crossed my mind that I was going to leave. There were a number of scenarios of what could have happened – First, Second or Third Division – but I had made my mind up, and consulted with my family because at the time my girlfriend was pregnant, but at no point did I think I would be leaving.

Wallace's early mention of his impending fatherhood and the desire to do the best by his family appears to have been a major factor in his decision, and he talks openly about the need for a balance between private and professional life:

> It was certainly a bit of both, the balance was there... I wanted to make things as comfortable as possible for when wee Leo was born, and I discussed it with my girlfriend. On the playing side of things, the hunger to win things at this club still remained regardless of where we were

going be playing our football. I still wanted to try and win something here and hopefully it can still happen.

But staying with Rangers has been to the detriment of his international career. Does he regret that side of things at all? He is very assertive in his answer:

> Missing out on Scotland, if that's due to me playing in the lower leagues then I just need to accept that. My sole focus has always been on doing well for Rangers and the international thing would only come as a bonus. It was always about Rangers. If I lost out on international football, then I would just accept that.

It is an early spring day and the sun is shining on the pitches outside. It really does look like a great place to work on a daily basis. Even the man at the reception desk is friendly and helpful to a fault. My escort for the day is Carol Patton from the press office, and she has asked me three times in the space of five minutes if I want tea or coffee. She shouts over Ian Durrant to introduce us and basically does everything she can to make the day go smoothly. Yet she, with so many others, faced losing her job when the CVA proposal was rejected by HMRC. You can sense the issue is still thorny, even Durrant rolls his eyes and curses at the mention of what I'm writing about. Wallace himself had come from a club where players' wages were regularly late and must have thought he had arrived somewhere that offered a bit more security. So how did it feel when his dream move turned sour and the club announced it was going into administration:

> It was a bit of a gutter obviously, for everyone. No-one saw it coming to a club the size of Rangers, so it was a bit of a tough one to take. There were a couple of months of not knowing what was happening; going into administration, taking the cuts – they weren't great times. The football had a dip at that period but I'd like to think that the guys that are still here and were involved in that period have come out it stronger – and that's the manager and staff included.
>
> It was hard in terms of how long it went on. We had a number of meetings in here with the PFA to see if we could come to an agreement with what was going on with the Administrators. There were a number of meetings up the stairs and it dragged on a bit. We were obviously just wanting to get things fixed as quickly as possible, but the problems higher up dictated otherwise and that things would be a bit more prolonged.

I point out the family feel to the place and ask Wallace if there was a concerted effort during the administration process and negotiations to save as many non-playing jobs as possible:

> I think so. Obviously we were all trying to get resolved as a club
> together. A huge part in taking the cuts was obviously to keep people
> in a job; whether it was at Ibrox or here [Murray Park]. We all collec-
> tively came to a decision to do all we could to keep everyone together.

Obviously the negotiations were successful as no non-playing staff lost
their jobs, but the club was unable to keep 'everyone together' due to
the refusal of some players to transfer over. I point out that this was an
alien feeling as a Rangers supporter: to watch players abandon the club
so ruthlessly. 'It was alien to us as well' is his frank assessment of my
feelings on the issue:

> The players that left, there is no denying they are top players and
> brought success to the club over the last two, three, four years. For the
> ones that were involved last season – myself, Jig, Neilly and a few of
> the younger boys – it was a bit alien when they chose to move on.

So what about the future, does he see himself being here until the job is
done and Rangers are back in the top tier of Scottish football, qualifying
for the Champions League and vying for trophies again?

> Absolutely! This season has been the first stage in our journey back to
> where we all want to be. There have been ups and downs but the main
> objective at the start of this season was to win this league. Hopefully,
> with whatever is happening with league reconstruction, we do move on.
> The objective set out was to win that league and keep moving and growing
> as a club. We all want to be back playing European nights and playing
> at the top level where Rangers should be. For everyone here, that's the
> main objective.
>
>   The manager has got everything running here as professional as it
> has been since I joined the club. The training is possibly harder in terms
> of intensity and workload than it was last season, albeit the standard
> maybe isn't as high because the players we lost were all top players. I
> think we can all hold our hands up and say the standard hasn't been the
> same, but the training intensity and workload, for me personally, has
> been every bit as hard, if not harder than last season and the manager
> would never allow things to be any different.

His last comments reassure in the face of accusations, based on a string of
unconvincing performances, that the standard of the training regime has
slipped. But Wallace is resolute in his defence of his club, manager and
team mates. He comes across as a settled veteran despite only being at
Ibrox for a couple of years. He gives the impression of someone who
wants to be here a long time:

I'll take everything as it comes. Football is a strange game but there is no doubt I want to try and help this football club get back to where we belong. Like a number of guys, I see myself being here for a long time.

It's a great place to come and play football and train. The facilities are first class. Going to play at Ibrox every second week is tremendous, so there is no better place to be playing. We're on the first steps of recovery in this league and I certainly want to be here as we grow and get back to where we belong.

It comes through quite strongly that Wallace has been bitten by the bug. That the club has had that infectious, under your skin effect that so many talk about. I point to his first sentence in the interview where he mentioned coming to a dressing room that was full of 'winners'. On the wall of the main corridor outside the room we're sitting in there is a line of framed winning cup final jerseys, the only runners-up one being the UEFA Cup final jersey from 2008. So did wanting to be a winner have a bearing on his decision to stay at the club? Is it all about being a winner?

Exactly. That's what's been installed at this club; there has always been a winning mentality. That expectancy has obviously been put on our shoulders this season and you've always got the success of recent years creeping over your shoulder. But that's something that comes with the territory of being a Rangers player, and it's been installed in us. We all want to be winners and hopefully we can become winners of this league, which I'll take with great pride because, although it's the Third Division, I've always said winning anything with this club is first class.

Wallace shoots off at this point for treatment and then training. He has reassured me that playing for Rangers is still a big deal. The club has had a torrid time of it. Some players exploited that, but others remained committed to club and its efforts to bring the glory days back. I am still a little bit suspicious of the modern day footballer – but Wallace has represented his kind, not to mention himself and the club, very well.

As I make my way out of Auchenhowie, I stop to look at the aforementioned framed strips on the wall representing various successes. I point out to the man at the reception desk that they are rapidly running out of room.

'Aye', he barks back, 'hopefully we'll run out of walls.'

CHAPTER V

Taking on the Establishment: Rangers and the Scottish Football Authorities

CHRIS GRAHAM

ONE OF THE most striking aspects of the story of Rangers' fall and rise, but one which has not been examined in enough detail, is the role played by the Scottish football authorities. As discussed elsewhere in this book, the amount of lobbying against Rangers by rival fans and elements of the press has taken Rangers fans, perhaps naively, by surprise. What could not reasonably have been foreseen was the adversarial stance taken by both the Scottish Football Association (SFA) and the Scottish Premier League (SPL) towards the club. Both Rangers and the Rangers fans had a right to assume that the football authorities in Scotland would assist a member club in trouble. But in reality, the only football body in Scotland to actually stand beside the club, despite Rangers not even being a member of their organisation until after the event, was the Scottish Football League (SFL).

With the confusion, and at times mayhem, which surrounded Rangers during the period from February 2012 to the present, it is sometimes easy to forget the catalogue of blows that were dealt to the already damaged club by the football authorities themselves. When one looks back at the myriad ways in which the club was further weakened by what the fans saw as the incompetence, maliciousness and indecision of those in charge of our game, it is truly shocking.

The alarm bells started to ring quite early on. In contrast with the English authorities' approach to clubs in financial distress like Portsmouth, there were very few comforting sound bites coming from the corridors of power in Hampden with regard to Rangers' situation. In fact what emerged was an almost insatiable wish to punish the club to the full extent of the rules, and beyond, and not only to inflict, but to be seen to be inflicting, maximum damage on an already ailing Scottish institution. Much of this was driven by the pressure applied by vested interests, from rival fans to certain SPL club chairmen, but this should not be seen as a defence. The SFA in particular had a duty to be above this type of lobbying but they could not separate themselves from the feeding frenzy which engulfed the club.

It is perhaps easier to see the contrast if we first examine the case of Portsmouth, which bears a contemporary comparison to the Rangers case. On 7 March 2012, with Portsmouth struggling to pay players in order to meet its remaining fixtures for that season, the Football League released £800,000 worth of payments to them. These took the form of £200,000 monthly payments which allowed the club to carry on and were made despite rules stating that these types of payments should be frozen in the event of administration. It was reported that the Football League, 'in recognising the severity of Portsmouth's plight' agreed to release the payments despite having no obligation to do so.[1]

What we've seen in the case of Portsmouth is a benevolent football authority dealing with a member club not according to the dictates of negative fan pressure, media frenzy or even stringent enforcement of their own rules, but in a sensible and pragmatic way which is designed purely to avoid that club's financial situation becoming more serious. It is worth noting that there has not been the same campaign from rival fans, sections of the media, or rival clubs to harm Portsmouth, and therefore the Football League was under less pressure to make an example of them, but their actions act as a stark reminder of the absurd approach of the SPL and SFA to Rangers.

When Rangers entered administration they were immediately docked ten points by the SPL under their existing rules. I have seen very few grumbles about this from Rangers fans. The rules were clear on this matter and the punishment was accepted despite it effectively handing the title to Celtic. It was after this initial punishment that things started to go awry. The SFA were first to enter the fray. Within a week of Rangers going into administration they had announced that an inquiry would look into the conduct of the club and Craig Whyte. The inquiry was chaired by Lord Nimmo Smith and Stewart Regan, the CEO of the SFA, was included on the panel along with Bob Downes, Deputy Chairman of the Scottish Environmental Protection Agency and Professor Niall Lothian, Past President of the Institute of Chartered Accountants of Scotland. Within two weeks it had completed its investigation into potential breaches of the

---

Articles of Association of the SFA and had submitted a report to the SFA board.

On 8 March, only a month after Rangers had entered administration and during a crucial period in which Duff & Phelps were attempting to find a buyer for the club, Regan announced that the SFA board considered Whyte not to be a fit and proper person to run Rangers and that the club and Whyte would face a disciplinary tribunal to determine any punishments for these alleged breaches.

The tribunal went ahead a month later and after hearing four days of evidence from Lord Nimmo Smith's report, it imposed a £160,000 fine on the club, still in administration, and a year-long registration embargo which meant Rangers would be barred from signing any players over the age of 18 to replace the 20 or so first team squad players who would leave the club.

The sense of injustice at this decision was acute. The rules clearly stated that the SFA had the right to impose financial penalties on the club but vague charges of 'bringing the game into disrepute' meant very little to suffering fans and added to the feeling that the SFA were making it up as they went along. Fines were levied at their maximum despite the club making a compelling case that Whyte's actions should be separated from those of the club and in the context of administration, it seemed absurd to impose additional financial burdens. The registration embargo had come out of nowhere – a sanction levied at the whim of the tribunal and one which would have a material effect on those considering purchasing the club, given that they were effectively hamstrung from rebuilding the playing squad.

Rangers fans took to the streets in outrage – an unprecedented event which flies in the face of the sombre, staunch caricature of the club's fans. Those who once scoffed at their city rivals preponderance for gathering in the Parkhead car park to voice their dissent suddenly found themselves galvanised. Club employee and former player Sandy Jardine, led a peaceful march, of what the police estimated was around 10,000 Rangers fans, through the streets of the south side of Glasgow to the steps of Hampden, the national stadium and home of the SFA and SPL. Jardine delivered a speech to the crowd in which he spoke of how:

> the supporters want to demonstrate a united front and show the feeling over disgraceful decisions against our club.[2]

---

[2] 'Rangers fans march on Hampden and vow "action" against other clubs', *The Herald*, 28 April 201 23

Following this, the club predictably appealed and, equally predictably, the appeal was rejected by another SFA tribunal.

Rangers were left with no option but to take the matter to the Court of Session, a move publicly criticised by the SFA and almost everyone else not connected with the club. Many people, including myself on my personal blog, attempted to explain that simply having legal minds involved in SFA tribunals was no guarantee that the SFA were complying with the law because they were operating within a framework introduced, with much fanfare, by Regan. The tribunal system was put together to deal with disputes over players being sent off and managers saying a little too much about referees. It was not designed to deal with complex matters of football governance and law and was to fall at its first attempt to deal with such matters.

This viewpoint was publicly derided by many rival bloggers and also on social media by mainstream journalists like Graham Spiers of *The Herald* and BBC. It turned out, however, that those who had pointed out the flaws in the SFA tribunal reasoning were correct. On the 29 May, Lord Glennie ruled in the Court of Session that the registration embargo was not an available punishment and that it could not be enforced. The SFA's response to this ruling, which made a mockery of their new tribunal process, was to publicly attack Rangers for not taking the matter to the Court of Arbitration for Sport (CAS) prior to seeking judicial review:

> No representation was made by the club to the Scottish FA to discuss the possibility or the process of seeking arbitration via the Court of Arbitration for Sport before Judicial Review was actioned.[3]

This was despite the fact that, in his judgement, Lord Glennie made it clear that this route was not open to Rangers and that CAS would not have heard the case.

At the time of all these various tribunals and appeals, the Administrators were trying to find a buyer. From the Blue Knights to Bill Miller, from Bill Ng to Brian Kennedy, every single prospective buyer criticised the sanctions hanging over the club. They highlighted their frustration that, without the resolution of these issues, they could not even be sure the club would be able to play the following season and liabilities could not be measured.

Including the appeals, the whole process took over three months.

---

[3] 'Charles Green and SFA argue over Rangers' Civil Court route', BBC Sport Website, 3 June 2012

The SFA kept the threat of sanction hanging over the club throughout the entire administration process and, indeed, right up until a day before the season started. Regan continued to defend the SFA's actions, stating that they had employed the 'strongest legal brains in the country'. He also maintained the 'independence' of the tribunals despite the members having been chosen by the SFA and having to operate within the framework of the SFA's rules which, on this occasion, had been shown to be at odds with Scots Law.[4]

The SPL were also doing their bit to make life as difficult for the club as possible. They made it clear through the media, soon after Rangers went into administration, that new rules would be brought in to sanction clubs who went into administration and emerged with a NewCo structure – the preferred method for several prospective Rangers bidders. The proposed rule changes were to give higher points deduction penalties for administration than the ten point penalty already suffered by Rangers and also to impose penalties for exiting administration through the formation of a NewCo. It was proposed that, on formation of a NewCo, clubs should incur ten point penalties for two years following the transfer of their SPL licence and a reduction in SPL income due to that club of 75 per cent for those two years.

This had the effect of creating further uncertainty amongst bidders as the imposition of these penalties would have effectively rendered Rangers impotent in challenging for the title for two years and significantly reduced their income during that period. Several bidders attempted to seek clarification from the SPL on whether the proposed sanctions were likely to be applied to Rangers but the SPL procrastinated. Despite announcing several meetings to discuss the subject, they delayed voting on these proposed sanctions on both 30 April and 7 May 2012. It was after the initial postponement that Neil Doncaster (SPL CEO), in attempting to play down the possible impact on the bidding process, uttered words which should now be infamous given the litany of sanctions that were to follow for Rangers:

> You may not be aware that, for example, Plymouth Argyle and Crystal Palace were also NewCos when they came out of administration and they emerged without any sanction at all.[5]

4 Stephen McGowan, 'Rangers are on their own, says SFA CEO Regan', *Mail Online*, 7 June 2012

5 Hugh McDonald, 'A decision is coming but when it may be made is anyone's guess', *The Herald*, 1 May 2012

The SPL clubs reconvened on 30 May but, instead of voting through the proposed fixed sanctions, again fudged the issue. They concluded that it would be better to decide sanctions on a 'case by case basis'. This meant that the remaining 11 SPL clubs would decide, amongst themselves, how to deal with a NewCo Rangers. There were, theoretically, any number of penalties available to them, including the one they ultimately took which was to reject the application to transfer the SPL share to the new company running the club. This bizarre decision, which provided no clarity on the subject and left Rangers facing ad hoc punishment at the whim of jealous, rival clubs, was described by Neil Doncaster as a 'very bold step'.

During all this mayhem, to which both the SFA and SPL greatly contributed, Charles Green had incredibly agreed a deal with the Administrators, Duff & Phelps, to purchase the club either through a Company Voluntary Arrangement (CVA) or, if that failed, to use a NewCo structure to complete the purchase via a sale of assets. The CVA was rejected by HMRC on 12 June and Charles Green announced that the NewCo route would be taken to allow the club to rebuild. This left Rangers at the mercy of the 11 other SPL clubs.

What followed is perhaps the lowest point for the football authorities in this entire saga although it has strong competition. They set about issuing dire warnings about the consequences of what were effectively their own actions. The SPL board heaped pressure on the SFL to parachute Rangers into the First Division – a move which would lessen the financial impact on the SPL of Rangers' absence, as it would effectively only last for one year, but would allow them to pander to the vocal sections of their fan bases who demanded Rangers removal from the top flight of Scottish football.

Both Stewart Regan and Neil Doncaster issued veiled threats of the financial implications if the SFL did not comply. Fans took to internet message boards to warn the 11 SPL club chairmen that they would vote with their feet if Rangers were allowed to continue in the SPL. Season ticket boycotts were threatened. Promises were made of increased attendances at games if the chairmen did the 'right thing' and cast Rangers into the Scottish football wilderness. This 'No to NewCo' movement, which has since turned out to be a sham with reduced attendances or revenues across all SPL clubs, lobbied chairmen to vote Rangers out of the league but not without a little help from Stewart Regan.

The first few days of July saw feverish talks behind closed doors. It was clear the SFL clubs were being put under huge pressure to accept Rangers into the First Division and lessen the impact of removing them from the SPL. Turnbull Hutton, the Raith Rovers Chairman, was clear in his contempt for this approach. He contended:

> If we are at the stage of bending rules and accommodating, threatening and blackmailing, we want to give it up. There is a lot of pressure being applied on people. There's been an abdication of duty from the SPL. Now the Scottish FA wades in and it's being punted to the SFL to let them try and sort it out.[6]

On 3 July, an SFL briefing from Stewart Regan and Neil Doncaster provoked outrage amongst SFL chairmen. Clyde, for example, issued a statement in which they referred to the 'currently absent leadership of the SFA'. They were the first club to publicly state that Regan had indicated in the meeting that the SFA would veto any attempt to accept Rangers into the SPL by refusing to transfer their SFA membership:

> The SFA implication is that there will be no entry to the SPL. The SPL implication is that it therefore has to be SFL1 with a bit of restructure, or an SPL2 with the rest of the SFL cut adrift.

The same day, the Rangers Fans Fighting Fund (RFFF) published the results of a poll which confirmed what Rangers fans had been telling the football authorities for weeks. Seventy-five per cent of Rangers fans voted that the club should resume playing in the Third Division. An RFFF spokesman said:

> Every other club and their fan base seem to have had an opinion of what should happen to Rangers. That's why we wanted Rangers fans to voice their opinion – and they have done so. It shows the depth of feeling among our fans who have shown that they don't want any preferential treatment. What these Rangers fans are saying is: 'If that is what is to happen to us, then let it happen and let us move on. We will support Rangers – no matter where they are playing.'

On 4 July, the SPL clubs finally took the decision to remove Rangers from the SPL, clearly feeling that the SFL clubs had been beaten into submission and would accept the fudge demanded by Doncaster and Regan. However, the SFL clubs stood firm. More clubs issued statements heavily criticising the SPL and SFA handling of the matter. On 9 July, Morton joined Clyde, Raith and others in their outspoken criticism. The club's Chairman, Douglas Rae, sent a letter to the other SFL chairmen in which he asserted:

---

[6] 'Raith Rovers Chief slams SFA and SPL', *Daily Record*, 1 July 2012

Scottish Football League (SFL) clubs are being placed in an intolerable position by the SFA and the overwhelming decision by the SPL to refuse to admit NewCo Rangers into the Premier League.

Rae tore into Neil Doncaster's handling of the briefing a week earlier:

The SPL CEO made scant contribution other than trying to impress on clubs that if we did not vote Rangers into the SFL Division One, financial disaster of epic proportions would be the experience many clubs would suffer.

He reserved the most scathing comments for Regan, plainly accusing him of lying about his claims to the press that he had not threatened to veto any move to allow Rangers back into the SPL:

The most concerning point about Regan's presentation was he departed truth as he became increasingly desperate to get his viewpoints accepted. When asked what would have happened if SPL clubs had voted NewCo Rangers entry to the Premier League, he stated that the SFA would block it. I asked why that point had not been made known to the clubs prior to the meeting. Stuart [sic] stated that sometimes points are withheld until the last moment for greater effect. I asked, through the chair, if I could ask Regan to repeat what he had said about 'blocking'. He responded by repeating what he had said minutes before; namely that the SFA would block any result that would see NewCo Rangers entering the SPL. The following day Stuart [sic] countermanded in the press what he had told the SFL meeting the previous day. It is very disappointing the SFA chief executive was unable to give a truthful response to SFL chairmen.[7]

Finally, on 13 July, Rangers fate was known. The SFL clubs voted to admit Rangers into the Third Division. The rest should have been straightforward but again the SFA and SPL stepped in to complicate matters. The authorities demanded that Rangers accept a 'five way agreement' between the SPL, SFA, SFL and Rangers' old and new companies.

Two weeks of fraught negotiations took place until the club were finally forced into accepting a range of sanctions in order for the SFA to transfer their membership to the new company. Rangers had to accept the registration embargo, starting on 1 September 2012, despite it having been ruled legally unenforceable in the Court of Session. An SFA statement made it clear that they had forced the club into ignoring the ruling it had secured earlier that year:

7   Chris Tait, 'Morton Chairman launches scathing attack on Scottish football's top brass', *The Herald*, 9 July 2012

It has been agreed that the registration embargo will be accepted as a
primary condition of a transfer of membership.

Rangers also had to pay all outstanding fines and costs to the SFA,
including the costs for the Court of Session challenge to the registration
embargo, which the club won, and all outstanding football debt to clubs
both within and outwith Scotland. They also had to accept being part
of a hastily cobbled together deal to keep the Sky and ESPN television
contracts alive. This granted the broadcasters rights to show 15 Rangers
games as part of the SPL contract, with the SFL receiving a token sum to
be distributed to all their member clubs.

Furthermore, the SPL retained all prize money due to the club for their
second place finish the previous season and reserved the right to pursue
potential stripping of titles for the years in which Rangers had utilised
EBT loans to players. This last point in the agreement was to mean that
the ill feeling and mistrust, which had built up over the summer, was set
to continue for almost another nine months.

The SPL had announced on 18 June that Rangers had a *prima facie*
case to answer in respect of league rules over payments to players. This
followed an investigation by the law firm Harper Macleod, who, much
to the dismay and mistrust of Rangers fans, not only represented the SPL
but Rangers' city rivals, Celtic.

On 17 August, the SPL announced that an independent commission
had been appointed to consider the case against the club. It was to be
chaired by Lord Nimmo Smith who was joined by Charles Flint QC and
Nicholas Stewart QC. This panel was initially scheduled to sit in October
but was delayed until 13 November due to uncertainty over the date of
the 'Big Tax Case' result, which was to have a material bearing on the
outcome. The hearing was then further delayed due to an injury, sustained in a car crash, to Rod McKenzie of Harper Macleod, a man seen
by the SPL as crucial to their chances of success.

The role of Harper Macleod was a source of constant debate
throughout this part of the Rangers story. A glowing testimonial from
Celtic CEO Peter Lawwell, which was hastily removed from the Harper
Macleod website, did the rounds of social media sites and internet message boards along with rumours that McKenzie had been particularly
confrontational in his dealings with Rangers during negotiation over the
'five way agreement' in the summer.

Questions arose over not only Harper Macleod's links to Celtic but
also their involvement in preparing the case against the club whilst also

being responsible for answering questions for the commission on the interpretation of the SPL's rules. The SPL eventually responded to questions on these conflicts of interest with a weak assertion that Harper Macleod's role was simply that of 'low level' paper gathering.[8] That the SPL then twice delayed the hearing, due to the injury sustained by McKenzie, a partner in the firm, made a mockery of this assertion. At a time of great financial hardship for the SPL, the fact they were willing to spend an estimated £400,000 on the case against Rangers was testament to the verve with which some clubs wanted to pursue the matter. It was notable that an EBT scheme for Celtic's Juninho was dealt with quietly and internally by the SPL, with Celtic being cleared after a brief examination by SPL Operations Director, Iain Blair.

During what became a six month wait for the commission hearing, details also emerged of an early draft of the 'five way agreement' which clearly showed that the SPL and SFA attempted to force Rangers into accepting the stripping of five SPL titles, won during the time EBTs were used. This attempt was resisted by the club and did not end up forming part of the agreement, but was seen by Rangers as evidence that the SPL had predetermined both guilt and sanction.

The commission finally convened on 29 January 2013 and heard several days of evidence. Rangers refused to take part, citing their misgivings over the attempt to include title stripping in the five way agreement. The Rangers Fans Fighting Fund stepped in, however, and funded a lawyer and QC to contest the charges on behalf of the old company in what was ultimately a successful move.

On 28 February 2013 the commission gave their verdict and, despite being found to have not properly disclosed the details of EBT loans to players, the club was only censured for these administrative omissions and given a £250,000 fine, levied on the Rangers OldCo. The commission acknowledged that, with the OldCo going through liquidation, this fine was a token punishment. The commission cleared the club of any attempt to cheat or to gain a competitive advantage from the use of EBTs:

> Rangers FC did not gain any unfair competitive advantage from the contraventions of the SPL rules in failing to make proper disclosure of the side-letter arrangements, nor did the non-disclosure have the effect that any of the registered players were ineligible to play, and for this

---

8   Stephen McGowan, 'Rangers boss McCoist fears SPL vendetta over EBT scheme after Juninho Celtic verdict', *Mail Online*, 14 September 2012

and other reasons no sporting sanction or penalty should be imposed upon Rangers FC.[9]

The result saw the SFA and SPL come under renewed pressure over the attempt to force the club into accepting title stripping in the summer of 2012. Regan and Doncaster were criticised in the press but still appeared to remain Teflon coated. It has been a feature of both the SPL and SFA media approach to the Rangers crisis that in times of heavy criticism they retreat to their Hampden bunker to wait out the storm. This has been, much to the frustration of Rangers fans, largely successful. That these organisations remain intact with the same people leading them, despite public allegations of lying and blackmail, is as much an indictment of the persistence of the Scottish press and broadcast media as it is of the organisations themselves.

It is perhaps ironic that it may be the failure of the authorities to bring about many rival fans desired outcome for Rangers that will be their undoing. Despite them offering the club no assistance and seemingly acting at almost every turn to hinder the recovery of Rangers, the club has survived and is beginning to rebuild. The pressure on the SFA and SPL is now coming not only from Rangers fans, dismayed at their treatment of the club, but from fans of other clubs incensed that Rangers have endured and retained their world record 54 titles.

Rival fans, some SPL club chairmen and the general public had become so conditioned to the idea that Rangers had cheated, that SPL titles would be stripped and that the club would be disgraced, that many are now turning their frustration on Neil Doncaster and Stewart Regan because this desired outcome has not been achieved. It seems impossible that they will survive with their jobs intact but I wrote the same in a *Scotland on Sunday* column[10] in the summer of 2012 and they defied the odds.

At the time of writing, there is another social media campaign forming to attempt to rewrite history and suggest that Doncaster and Regan should be removed not because of the way they treated Rangers but because they gave the club too much assistance. This assertion is utterly baseless but facts tend not to get in the way of these types of campaigns.

So what of Rangers? How do the club and the fans move forward from here after their relationship with the authorities has been so badly

---

[9] 'Rangers: SPL Commission will not strip club of SPL titles', BBC Sport website, 28 February 2013

[10] Chris Graham, 'Regan's success is to unite fans in calling for his resignation', *Scotland on Sunday*, 7 July 2012

compromised? There is no doubt that a huge amount of ill feeling and mistrust still exists. The football authorities were given a huge problem to deal with and it was not their fault that Rangers found themselves in the financial position they did. It was not their fault that the club slipped into administration and that it ultimately had to emerge through the NewCo route. It is also true to say that the club could not be allowed to escape without sanction. Craig Whyte's actions during his short term in charge, despite not being in line with the traditions, values or wishes of the club, had to be seen to be punished. However, the scale of the punishment, the timing of the action taken and the length of time taken to reach conclusions on the various investigations was scandalous.

We are now in a position where it is entirely possible that the people involved in the ruin of Rangers may find themselves in the dock. Craig Whyte, Gary Withey (the Collyer Bristow partner who worked with Whyte on the takeover) and others have serious questions to answer and, at the time of writing, police investigations are well underway. The liquidators, BDO, also have wide ranging powers of investigation into the financial plundering of the club during Craig Whyte's short lived but disastrous reign.

Would it have been impossible for the SFA to delay their tribunals and sanctions until these investigations were complete? Surely everyone would have benefitted from knowing more about what unfolded in the months before the club went into administration before deciding what punishment was required? The new company was forced to pay the fines and costs of the OldCo anyway, it was forced to pay outstanding transfer fees and prize money was withheld by the SPL. Why was there such a clamour to impose sanctions before the matter was properly investigated?

The title stripping attempt by the SPL has probably left the most residual bitterness. Fans understandably find it much harder to accept the attempted removal of trophies, won through hard work and sporting excellence, than they do the payment of fines. It was against every principle of natural justice for the SPL and SFA to attempt to remove Rangers' titles without first proving any guilt but that is precisely what they did. 'Sporting Integrity' was a phrase both misused and overused during the summer of 2012 by those seeking to inflict maximum damage on Rangers. There was no integrity, sporting or otherwise, on display from the football authorities during this episode.

It has scarcely been mentioned that the authorities knew of the existence of the HMRC investigation into EBTs as early as October 2010 when HMRC first made enquiries about whether the EBTs had been registered with them. Why did it take them almost a year and a half, and Rangers entering administration, to open an investigation into the affair? They waited until the club was at its lowest point, and in complete disarray, to challenge the use of the scheme. It may just have been incompetence but perhaps some, particularly within the SPL, saw it as an opportunity too good to miss.

There is also a feeling that the SFA in particular were far too easily influenced by outside forces in their treatment of the club. The SPL is a hive of self-interest. Neil Doncaster serves the clubs who make up the top league. He is not there to look after Scottish football as a whole but Stewart Regan and the SFA are. The contrast between the concessions afforded to clubs in England who find themselves in financial difficulties and the way in which Rangers were dealt with is stark.

On 7 March 2013 it was reported that Dunfermline had received advanced payments of monies due from the SFA in order to attempt to keep the club going against a backdrop of serious financial difficulties. When they finally entered administration later in the year, they escaped an SFA tribunal with no fine and a six month registration embargo. The optimist would say that perhaps this is a sign that the SFA have learnt from their mistakes. The more cynical might say they are under less pressure to be seen to deal severely with a smaller club and therefore more likely to lend assistance.

Only the SFL, and their Chief Executive, David Longmuir, have emerged from this story with any credit. Longmuir and the SFL board have consistently dealt with the club fairly and sensibly whilst upholding the integrity of their competitions. They have done so whilst maintaining a clear view of what is necessary to benefit all the clubs in the SFL. The SFL were the first to publicly state that they would not support the attempt to strip titles from the club. The League Cups won by Rangers during the EBT years were never under threat due to the SFL's principled stance that retrospective attempts to remove them, with no evidence of cheating, would be outrageous. Longmuir stated:

> From the day we announced that Rangers would be in the Third Division my only thought was how to rebuild the game, get investment back in and take the game forward. I'm not looking back any more. I'm getting to the point now where I can see light at the end of the tunnel and I can see the game beginning to get back on its feet.[11]

---

[11] Michael Grant, 'SFL rule out stripping Rangers of League Cups won during EBT era', *The Herald*, 21 July 2012

The club was weakened by years of overspending, it was mugged and left for dead by Craig Whyte, but instead of helping it back onto its feet, the football authorities seemed more intent on rifling the pockets of the victim. History is unlikely to judge those involved favourably but the concern for the game as a whole is that the same structure and leadership remain in place despite their woeful mishandling of the events of the past 18 months.

Perhaps there will be an opportunity for principled, honest men like David Longmuir to take a more prominent role in the governance of the Scottish game. We can only hope so, because something will have to change if the game is to be rejuvenated and if trust is to be rebuilt between one of Scotland's largest clubs and those tasked with overseeing the game in this country.

CHAPTER VI

Succulent Lamb or Inaccurate Spam? Rangers and the Media

CHRIS GRAHAM

THERE IS NO question that the media interest in Rangers over the past two years has been more intense than ever. The club has been accustomed to a massive amount of coverage in Scotland and, at times of success, around the UK and Europe. However, the level of interest in the past 18 months has become markedly greater due initially to the financial troubles of the club and then, more recently, the coverage of our rise out of the financial mire and the fans' part in that. There have been positive stories worldwide, from the USA to Australia, but in our own country, Scotland, it seems that Rangers are still trapped in negativity.

As a Rangers fan it seemed over the summer of 2012, and still seems, as if the media has done its utmost to project a prejudicial and negative view of the club to the public. To this day, despite the favourable results in almost every investigation in which Rangers have been involved, there is still a perception amongst the general public that the club has 'cheated' or acted 'immorally'. This perception has sprung from media coverage which has been all too eager to judge the club prior to the outcome of the various tribunals and court cases in which it has been involved. This has been the responsibility of various media outlets, from the BBC with Mark Daly's *The Men Who Sold the Jerseys* documentary and their news and radio output, to the erratic press coverage from, at times, hostile hacks. This chapter cannot cover the whole range of media output on Rangers over this period but it will examine some key contributions.

There are three main areas of contention concerning the media coverage of the club. First was the presumption of guilt both in the 'Big Tax Case' (BTC) and the SPL tribunal into 'dual contracts' or 'side letters'. This was not only prejudicial to the public perception of the club but could also be seen to have directly affected the Scottish football authorities' approach. Second was the coverage of the results of the BTC and SPL tribunals which, when the verdicts went against the predicted outcome, were met with denial and in some instances outright hostility. Finally there were attempts to promote Rangers as a 'new club' despite confirmation from various official footballing bodies, courts and tribunals that this was not the case.

There is no question that the Scottish media were playing catch up with the *Rangers Tax Case* (RTC) blog in reporting the early stages of Rangers' financial demise and their use of EBTS. The blog, despite its barely concealed hatred for the club, appears to have had inside information. I do not want to say too much about this, as the question of how that information was obtained is, at the time of writing, the focus of a police investigation but I will say that the success of the blog seemed to spur the media in general to take a considerably more adversarial approach to Rangers – almost as if they had to be seen to be making up for lost ground. Clearly they did not want to be beaten to the punch again and when the blog became more high profile, sections of the media took every opportunity to portray the club in as poor a light as possible. There was a willingness from many to accept the content and opinion of the blog as fact, with no pause to consider its agenda or its selective reporting of one side of a complex case.

Let us look first at the presumption of Rangers' guilt. All of the examples given below appeared prior to either the result of the Big Tax Case, which the club won, or the SPL tribunal which cleared the club of gaining any sporting advantage from the use of EBTS.

Alex Thomson of *Channel 4 News*, who we will return to in more detail later, attacked the club and the brand:

> Rangers now means a revolting broth of tax-evasion; threatening corporate aggression; a profoundly arrogant refusal to apologise ever to anyone for anything; a 'case to answer' on years of organised cheating; the brand name liquidated; the British taxpayer cheated; hundreds of small Scottish businesses, charities, colleges, councils out of pocket.[1]

Ewing Grahame, a freelance journalist who writes for *The Telegraph* and *The Sun* amongst others, made spurious claims of illegality, something which the club was never under investigation for:

> Rod McKenzie of Harper McLeod [*sic*], the sports law specialist who represents the SPL, believes that Rangers have a 'case to answer' over the use of dual contracts to players, a serious breach of regulations (not to mention the law of the land) which, on its own, could warrant expulsion.[2]

---

[1] Alex Thomson, 'How to detoxify the Rangers brand', Channel 4 News Website, 23 June 2012

[2] Ewing Grahame 'Rangers could be reborn, then gone, on the 4th July', *The Telegraph*, 18 June 2012

Hugh Keevins, of the *Daily Record* and Radio Clyde, appeared to refuse to even consider the idea that Rangers might be innocent of the charges made against them:

> An independent commission will decide which titles Rangers will lose over the dual contracts system that gave them an unfair advantage over opponents.[3]

Keevins, not content with simply foisting his own view on Rangers' guilt on us, was also busy reporting Celtic's view on the matter. Neil Lennon wasn't shy in telling us that he wanted Rangers stripped of titles despite no guilt having been established. Speaking in Germany, Lennon said:

> If they are stripped of titles so be it. It will be a moral victory for those who were treated unfairly. It won't change my life but it's right to do it for historical reference. What went on in the past cost players new contracts and bonus money. It might have helped relegate some clubs and cost managers their jobs.[4]

It is worth noting that both these articles from Keevins came on the same day. It seemed that he was just portraying Celtic's view on the proceedings. They wanted titles stripped and therefore so did Keevins. There was no doubt about Rangers' guilt; no qualification of Lennon's ranting with a line about how he might be wrong in his presumption of guilt.

Jim Spence was another particularly interesting example of this media narrative, simply because of the hypocrisy he showed in his approach to Rangers. Spence, as well as regularly pontificating on BBC Radio Scotland about the punishments Rangers should receive, also writes a blog for the BBC Scotland website. When Dundee FC was in financial difficulty in 2010, Spence had this to say:

> With Dundee fighting for their very existence, their fans have been royally shafted – once by their own board, and now by the SFL board. It wasn't the fans who didn't pay the tax bill, but they're the ones who stand to lose their club. Because make no mistake, Dundee FC are very close to going out of business, and it wasn't the fans that put them in that position.[5]

---

3 Hugh Keevins, 'Probe into Rangers title wins to be carried out by independent commission', *Daily Record*, 19 July 2012

4 Hugh Keevins, 'Stripping Rangers of titles will be moral victory for those treated unfairly', *Daily Record*, 19 July 2012

5 Jim Spence, 'Dundee penalty is misguided and inappropriate', BBC Scotland website, 2 November 2010

Fast forward a couple of years and Spence's compassion for football fans and understanding of clubs in financial peril appeared to have disappeared:

> Rangers have behaved with a reckless disregard for the rules that everyone else is expected to abide by. What comes next could be a morality tale. Will it be *Real Politic* [*sic*], where moral judgement is set aside in favour of pure financial consideration? Or will Rangers be required to purge themselves in some accomodation [*sic*] with the Scottish Football League and work their way back up the divisions to emerge refreshed and renewed?[6]

You will note we had reference from both Lennon and Spence to the 'morality' of the club being in question. Their own morals appear not to include a belief in the concept of innocent until proven guilty. Spence was no longer appealing for pragmatism from the Scottish football authorities but strict adherence to the rules. Surely this change of approach was not just because it was Rangers?

It wasn't only during their day jobs that journalists engaged in this public flogging of the club. Several took to Twitter to, in some cases, reach a wider audience than their articles would. Graham Spiers was a prime example of this. He has over 45,000 followers; I very much doubt that number of people pay to read his articles. On several occasions, prior to the outcome of either the BTC or the SPL tribunal, Spiers had Rangers down as 'guilty'. In May 2012, he tweeted, 'I think EBTs were a form of cheating, yes. I'm very comfortable using that word'. On 6 August 2012, Spiers kindly replied to a Celtic fan questioning him on Rangers with, 'I've said it a million times mate – I think RFC guilty'.

'Guilty', 'cheating', 'morality' – these were the buzzwords for the media through a long summer for Rangers fans. I would have some sympathy for these journalists if they had been one-off comments, after all we were asking sports journalists to have an opinion on complex tax and legal matters which, frankly, many of them did not understand. However, against that backdrop, would it not have been sensible for them to take a more rounded view of the possible outcomes? I would also have had more sympathy if they had admitted their mistake after the event but many did not, even when afforded the opportunity. In fact, Spiers denied ever having claimed that the use of EBTs was 'cheating' during a live appearance on *Scotland Tonight* the day of the BTC result, despite the

---

6 Jim Spence, 'SPL Fair Play proposals spark stormy reaction', BBC Scotland website, 12 April 2012

offending tweets still being present on his timeline: 'I have never ever used the word cheating to describe the Big Tax Case'.[7]

In my opinion, probably the most prejudicial piece of reporting prior to the BTC result came from the BBC's Mark Daly in his documentary *The Men Who Sold the Jerseys*. The information used in the documentary is believed by many, including Sir David Murray, to have come from documents illegally obtained from Her Majesty's Revenue and Customs (HMRC). At the time of writing there is a police investigation being carried out into where the leak originated and how the information came to be in the possession of the BBC. Personal tax information was displayed in the programme and it appeared to deliberately present only the prosecution, and ultimately the losing, side of an extremely complex case.

Daly, as you would expect, has defended his role but despite winning a Royal Television Society prize for the programme, the BTC win for Rangers and the favourable judgement of Lord Nimmo Smith in the SPL tribunal have made a mockery of the claims presented. What it did well was to further influence public opinion against the club. Based on claims made in the programme, which was essentially a dramatised regurgitation of the *Rangers Tax Case* blog, fans of other Scottish clubs felt they were informed about the level of non-payment of tax, that so called 'side letters' were against SPL rules and that the club had effectively been cheating. These claims have been repeated *ad nauseum* by many in the media and by online bloggers attached to other clubs, despite having been proven to be inaccurate.

This clamour to find the club guilty prior to any hearings was bad enough, but it was reasonable to assume that this would be toned down once Rangers won the First Tier Tax Tribunal. That was not the way it turned out however. Such was the belief in Rangers' guilt that the focus in the days after the result, which cleared Rangers of owing figures which the press had wrongly reported as being as high as £160m, was not on the verdict but on the dissenting opinion of Dr Heidi Poon, one of the tribunal members.

Despite a majority verdict clearing Rangers, her long and detailed dissenting opinion was the focus of several articles, as if journalists were trying to validate their own preconceptions and airbrush the actual result from history. Alex Thomson wrote a long blog quoting Poon extensively, and using her minority opinion as a basis to continue to link the club erroneously with 'cheating'.[8]

7 Graham Spiers, *Scotland Tonight*, 20 November 2012
8 Alex Thomson, 'Rangers: Were they cheating football, and the taxman?', *Channel 4 News* website, 4 December 2012

The Big Tax Case result was a particularly difficult pill to swallow for the RTC site. They got themselves into a complete mess by announcing Rangers had lost the case on the day of the announcement, then back-tracked when they realised the mistake. Within a few days they had deleted the entire content of the blog. Unperturbed, however, many of their fellow bloggers moved on to the sure-fire victory that was due in the shape of the SPL tribunal into 'dual contracts' or 'side letters'. Many journalists in Scotland followed suit. After all, Rangers had to be guilty of something surely?

This was the one remaining chance that this determined group of Rangers bashers had of getting something right. It was not to be. Rangers were unequivocally cleared of cheating and the outpouring of disappointment from many of the people mentioned above was palpable. Alex Thomson, from writing blogs extolling the credentials of the tribunal, and Lord Nimmo Smith in particular, suddenly felt the result was open to question. He went from:

> Lord Nimmo Smith has already had to put out a statement pointing out that he is independent and objective. It's rather like a polar bear pointing out that he's white and furry. Yet in Glasgow football, such things are deemed necessary in the miasma of suspicion that never lifts far from the Clyde.[9]

To the considerably less enthusiastic:

> Many will feel this is bizarre. The football world in Scotland had it as a bedrock belief that failure to disclose payment renders a player ineligible and that is that. Ergo: unfair advantage and thus cheating. Lord Nimmo Smith has ruled that this is not necessarily so and not so in this case – or cases. There will be many out there today who will see this as utterly bizarre, if not perverse.[10]

Thomson went a step further on an appearance on *Scotland Tonight* on 28 February 2013. It was actually quite amusing to note that the only title stripping which took place that day appeared to have been reserved for Lord Nimmo Smith himself. Having only previously referred to him using his title, Thomson seemed to decide he was no longer worthy of it

[9] Alex Thomson, 'Why Rangers face a massive re-writing of football club history', *Channel 4 News* website, 29 January 2013

[10] Alex Thomson, 'Rangers' player payments "not cheating"', *Channel 4 News* website, 28 February 20132

and persistently referred to him using his Christian name, William. Lord Nimmo Smith had become plain, old Billy.

Spiers took the line that Nimmo Smith's ruling stating Rangers had 'gained no competitive advantage' from the use of EBTs was 'in truth, the weakest part of his report'. He felt that:

> some in Scottish football will continue to be baffled by Nimmo Smith's conclusion in regard to no competitive advantage being gained by Rangers.

I think that for 'some in Scottish football' we can read, 'Celtic, Spiers and the other journalists who spent a year telling everyone Rangers had cheated'. He also felt that 'Nimmo Smith actually hedges his bets a little'.[11] This is nonsense, the ruling could not have been clearer, but is in keeping with the approach after the BTC verdict of clinging on to the parts of a complex judgement that back up your preconceived idea of the outcome and not reporting properly on the outcome itself.

If anything, the radio phone-in shows have been worse than the print media. The same cast of characters cajoling each other into even greater feats of stupidity and inaccuracy. BBC Radio Scotland has arguably been the worst, mainly because of their duty of impartiality. Spiers, Stuart Cosgrove and Spence are inclined towards a negative view of Rangers. That's fine, criticism can be healthy, but the BBC has a duty to balance its programming and, over the summer of 2012 and since, BBC Scotland have been seemingly unable to do so. It has not helped that the club refuse to cooperate with BBC Scotland after a number of incidents involving manager, Ally McCoist. One involved an interview with him being edited to make it look like he was laughing at the issue of sectarianism and another a *Mad Men* style montage in which McCoist appeared to be shown throwing himself from the top of Ibrox Stadium in order to commit suicide.

BBC Scotland have been the main protagonists in the 'new club' myth that has been put forward by those still mourning the survival of Rangers and its slow return to health. In the week of the one year anniversary of the OldCo going into administration, BBC Radio Scotland had two panel shows in which Rangers were described by those on the show as a new club. In the first, Jim Spence declared that Rangers were a new club 'although their fans would argue the toss'. The following night it was Spiers' turn to trot out this lazy, inaccurate and perhaps malicious line.

This idea that a new club has been formed is popular amongst Celtic

---

[11] Graham Spiers, 'Findings did not lead to stripping of titles but nor did they cover Rangers in glory', *The Herald*, 2 March 2013

fans for obvious reasons. They have frequently played second fiddle to Rangers and therefore see this as a way of catching up with the success of their rivals. Why supposedly impartial broadcasters would peddle the same line is less clear but it is hard to escape the conclusion that there is a level of vindictiveness involved. Both Spiers and Spence have been made aware of the SFA membership transfer to the new company that confirmed Rangers was the same club. They have been made aware of the European Club Association confirming Rangers' status as the same club. They should also be aware of an email sent to STV by UEFA which confirms they treat Rangers very specifically as a 'NewCo' – therefore confirming that they are the same club – in the same way that Leeds United are a NewCo and the same club. Not only have the football authorities confirmed it but so have several legal hearings and tribunals the club have attended. Lord Nimmo Smith stated:

> In common speech a Club is treated as a recognisable entity which is capable of being owned and operated, and which continues in existence despite its transfer to another owner or operator.
>
> It is the Club, not its owner and operator, which plays in the league.[12]

Lord Glennie also made clear the distinction between club and company when he said:

> This is a petition for judicial review by the Rangers Football Club PLC, a company presently in administration. That company presently operates Rangers Football Club (to whom I shall refer as 'Rangers')[13]

It is an odd thing to watch journalists ignore documented legal evidence that challenges their preconceptions, but that is what is happening regularly on BBC Radio Scotland, Radio Clyde and in sections of the press. Both Spiers and Spence 'feel' that Rangers are a new club. When you ask them to justify it they can't – it's just a feeling. Can you imagine a BBC newscaster or commentator telling us that they 'feel' someone is guilty despite a judge declaring them innocent? In my opinion, it is at best poor journalism and at worst deliberately dishonest.

It is not just on radio shows that BBC Scotland has featured this 'new club' myth. Since Rangers had their status confirmed by the SFA, with the membership transfer to the new company, BBC Scotland have printed no

[12] Lord Nimmo Smith, 'SPL Commission Reason for Decision', SPL website, 12 September 2012

[13] Lord Glennie, 'Opinion of Lord Glennie in petition of Rangers Football Club PLC', *Scotcourts.co.uk*, 6 June 2012

less than nine articles on their website claiming that Rangers are a 'new club'. This is factually incorrect but, despite this being pointed out regularly to them by irritated fans, the BBC continue to report it at regular intervals. This approach is in stark contrast to STV who, knowing that this was a sensitive topic, laid out very clear editorial guidelines to their staff. They identified that the SFA transfer of membership was the crucial indicator of the continuance of the club and ensured that, from the date of that transfer, Rangers would simply be referred to as Rangers.

It won't surprise you to learn that Ewing Grahame pops up again when we discuss the use of this 'new club' misdescription: 'Rangers, as a new club, are currently only associate members of the SFL'.[14] Even when reporting on Rangers winning the tax case, he couldn't help himself:

> The institution formerly known as Rangers Football Club has posthumously won its appeal against the tax bill presented to them in regard to its use of Employee Benefit Trusts (from 2001–10) during the tenure of former owner Sir David Murray. The new club owned by the aggregation of investors fronted by Charles Green.[15]

Never one to miss out on a bandwagon, Alex Thomson joins in too:

> The commission also distances the present new club set up from the ashes of the old liquidated club.[16]

It would be entirely wrong to say that all journalists took a confrontational or prejudicial stance towards the club. Richard Wilson of *The Herald* was a standout throughout the period, with well-informed articles which, whilst critical of the club at times, were well researched and always fair. Tom English of *The Scotsman*, seen by many fans as an outspoken critic of the club, was at least able to show glimpses of compassion. I probably disagree with 80 per cent of what English writes about the club, but he has never reserved his criticism for Rangers alone and has shown he is willing to take an equally critical line with Celtic – a rarity amongst the press in Scotland. STV's coverage was also generally excellent. Their team of journalists, including Peter Smith, Grant Russell and Andy Coyle, were willing and able to engage with fans on Twitter.

---

[14] Ewing Grahame, 'SFL face pressure as SPL clubs agree league changes', *The Scotsman*, 29 January 2013

[15] Ewing Grahame, 'Rangers win Big Tax Case appeal over use of Employee Benefit Trusts', *The Telegraph*, 20 November 2012

[16] Alex Thomson, 'Rangers' player payments 'not cheating'', *Channel 4 News* website, 28 February 2013

Whilst this often meant people disagreeing with them, they never hid from the debate.

STV also gave the Rangers story considerable airtime on the excellent *Scotland Tonight*, managing, in stark contrast to the BBC, to balance their panels. Whilst giving airtime to journalists who were prepared to be extremely critical, such as Graham Spiers and Tom English, they also allowed Rangers fans, and journalists who were more sympathetic to the plight of the club like Richard Wilson and Archie MacPherson, to enter the debate so it never became simply about sticking the boot in.

Another positive aspect of the media coverage was the response from overseas. Journalists flocked from every corner of the globe to hear about the story of the fans that turned up in their tens of thousands for Third Division games. It is a remarkable story of loyalty and support which those outside Scotland appeared to be able to grasp much more readily than our own country's media. I personally was interviewed by a Chinese TV station, an ESPN America documentary team, *The New York Times* (twice) as well as local media. Given the way our support had been battered by negativity about the club, I was always amazed at their interest and enthusiasm, but each and every one of them made a point of stating what an incredible response there had been from the fans. Whilst journalists in Scotland were making snide comments about 'defiance', those from around the world were talking about loyalty, fans who loved their club and the incredible desire of those fans to rebuild it.

Martin Ainstien, a documentary maker for ESPN, explained their interest in the story to me:

> We wanted to work on a story about Rangers because we felt it was not only an example of a club that has suffered the lack of financial control Europe has right now, but it demonstrated how important the club is for its real owners – the fans. Supporters realised there is no one more powerful than them to have a word on the club. This is a message for the rest of the world: *no one can take anything from you if you defend it with passion.* Rangers is a great story because it shows what football is about and because it shows a way out of a critical situation hundreds of clubs are suffering nowadays.

A Japanese journalist, Daisuke Nakajima, also explained the global interest in Rangers in an interview with the Rangers website:

> Even with Rangers now being in the Third Division, the crowds here are still so big and it is really interesting to us that everyone is still backing the team.[17]

---

[17] Andrew Dickson, 'Daisuke Gets His Story', *Rangers.co.uk*, 28 November 2012

Whilst foreign journalists were marvelling over the Rangers support, Hugh Keevins was doing his best to distort this loyalty as 'gullibility':

> Rangers' fans can't stop going to Ibrox in their tens of thousands to watch one-sided matches against wee teams who regard it a privilege to be ritually slaughtered. If they do they'll be mocked by Celtic supporters.[18]

Keevins' *Daily Record* stable mate was at it too. Gordon Waddell felt there was 'clearly money to be made in defiance'. He added:

> Fans are turning up in giant numbers – not because they love the Third Division but to prove that they are, in fact, The Peepil.[19]

These condescending comments were again made on the same day in the same paper. To be fair to Waddell, he has since retracted those comments and recognised the incredible loyalty the fans have shown. It is unfortunate that others who scoffed at and prodded the club, and fans, on a daily basis could not show the same humility.

Not every contribution from outside Scotland was a positive one. Alex Thomson's involvement in the Rangers story has been simplistic and superficial but certainly memorable. It was something of a surprise to see the *Channel 4 News* Chief Correspondent take such an interest in a football story and his involvement has never really been adequately explained. Thomson burst onto the scene with what he called an 'exclusive' interview with a former Rangers director, the late Hugh Adam. This interview was in fact a rehash of one which appeared in the *Daily Mail* a couple of weeks before and was uncomfortable viewing. A seriously ill Adam fumbled his way through questions and seemed to have words placed in his mouth by Thomson. His vague assertion that something was not right about Rangers' EBT scheme, despite him not ever having been directly involved in its administration, played some role not just in the public perception of Rangers' guilt, but also in the ensuing SPL investigation.

Thomson wrote his first blog on Rangers on 8 March 2012 and has written around 75 blogs during the period from then until 8 March 2013. It is almost certainly galling for Thomson that during that time he has received significantly more attention for his work on Rangers than he has on Syria, Northern Ireland and Afghanistan. One could certainly argue

---

[18] Hugh Keevins, 'Jibes are getting cheaper as seats for kids are getting dearer', *Daily Record*, 9 September 2012

[19] Gordon Waddell, 'Charles Green knows how to push fans buttons and it's making him money', *Daily Record*, 9 September 2012

that it is odd that the vast majority of ratings and comments on this blog are for a story about a football club but the figures don't lie. Thomson's profile has been substantially raised by reporting on Rangers despite him giving the impression that the whole thing was somewhat beneath him.

Thomson has, at almost every turn, although not uniquely, taken his lead on the Rangers story from the narrative created by sites like *Rangers Tax Case* and other Celtic-oriented blogs. He announced his disdain for the Scottish media early on in the process, citing the 'succulent lamb' culture of the press in Scotland and insinuating that Rangers got an easy ride because of it. This was almost a carbon copy of the approach taken by RTC and things continued in that vein. There are several instances of his reports appearing a couple of days after similar ideas have manifested themselves on the blogs of *Celtic Quick News* (CQN) or Phil Mac Giolla Bhain.

His focus on 'succulent lamb' comes from a now infamous story where certain Scottish journalists were invited to dinner with former Rangers owner Sir David Murray during which a couple commented on the quality of the lamb. It has become synonymous with the flawed idea that Rangers have the media in Scotland in their pocket. Thomson's biggest mistake with his regurgitation of this idea is that, if it was ever true, it is perhaps 20 years out of date. The notion that the Scottish press are in thrall to Rangers is absurdly easy to dispel, as we have seen.

Far from Thomson's claims of 'succulent lamb', a large section of the media in Scotland have been hostile to Rangers throughout the period of the past two years and, in reality, for many years previous. There have been many in the press who have barely been able to keep their reactions above the level of internet message boards. Not so much 'succulent lamb' as inaccurate spam.

Criticism of the media in this country tends to be met with scoffing, shouts of paranoia or sarcastic claims of conspiracy but it is complacency to suggest that tens of thousands of Rangers fans who are sick of the media reporting on the club have been gripped by some sort of mass delusion. These are not people howling at the moon. Many of those complaining are professional people who have felt compelled to start writing blogs and involving themselves in a defence of their club because they can see the dishonesty of some of the reporting. The challenges to organisations like BBC Scotland have been very specific and have a great deal of evidence to back them up.

Predictably, even the complaints themselves have been misrepresented by some. In one example, Graham Spiers attempted to put words in my mouth during an appearance on *Scotland Tonight* in which I mentioned the agenda in certain sections of the media to brand Rangers as guilty before any guilt had been established. He wanted to turn this into 'conspiracy' in order to dismiss it, but that was not the accusation. I think many journalists in this country have simply become comfortable slating Rangers in the same way that in the past others were perhaps comfortable never challenging the club. Neither is acceptable.

It has been easy in the past for journalists to ignore criticism but the emergence of sites like *The Rangers Standard* has made it more difficult for them to get away with this approach. Their one-sided views and the way they distort facts, or simply aren't aware of them, can be regularly challenged on a platform that is easily accessible to fans. Increasingly the younger generation of journalists in Scotland are taking notice of blogs and forming networks with enthusiastic amateurs. Often the standard of writing is considerably higher, and increasingly more informed, than some of the articles found in daily newspapers. Independent Rangers fan sites have even achieved higher readership for articles than those carried in national newspapers.

There is no question that the agenda in some sections of the media coloured public opinion, and made it not only much harder for the club to recover but also much easier for the football authorities and others to treat the club, and its fans, callously. Had it not been for the size of the Rangers fan base, and its willingness to stand up and be counted, then perhaps the club would not have prevailed – the irony being that without Rangers many of these journalists would not have a job.

There was a hysteria involved in the reporting on the club in 2012 and 2013. It has subsided somewhat but much of the damage has been done. You will struggle to find a fan of another club in Scotland who is not happy to repeat many of the myths created by the media over the past two years. In many people's eyes Rangers are still 'guilty' and have 'cheated' their way to titles. It will take a long time for the club to remove those stains and it is down, in large part, to a media who were all too willing to publicly flog the club prior to any of the cases against it being heard. Far from Rangers showing 'a reckless disregard for fair play'[20], I would charge sections of our media with showing a reckless disregard for fair and accurate reporting on a situation that, without their contribution, was already bringing the fans of Scottish football's pre-eminent club untold anguish.

---

[20] Graham Spiers, 'Expediency Trumps Justice', *The Herald*, 14 April 2012

CHAPTER VII

We Were the People

ALASDAIR MCKILLOP

THE RANGERS STORY boasted a long list of characters and some bizarre cameos but ultimately the most important people were the fans. They were the ones who avidly consumed reports detailing what was happening to their club and they were the ones who devoted their time and resources to nursing it through a period none of them were conditioned to imagine. At times, it felt as though these remarkable efforts were being given a begrudging acknowledgment by those who believe supporting Rangers is merely about success, defiance or, at worst, bigotry. Others seemingly ignored them completely and some even accused Rangers fans of having a dysfunctional culture that succours a dangerous underclass.[1]

Something clearly went badly wrong at Rangers. This was not the fault of the media, online bloggers or HM Revenue and Customs. An accumulation of poor decisions made by those responsible for ensuring the club's welfare was to blame. This is not to say there weren't those who revelled in the misfortunes of the club or even tried their utmost to maximise the damage inflicted. Although the crisis originated up the marble staircase at Ibrox, a number of professional bodies deserve to be scrutinised for the way they discharged their duties before, during and after the formal entry into administration of The Rangers Football Club PLC. Supporters were routinely and unfairly criticised for not acting to avert the disaster that befell their club. Such critiques conveniently overlooked the lack of convincing strategies available for the modern football fan to hold majority shareholders and billionaire owners to account. Over the years, however, Rangers fans displayed a tendency to conflate criticism of individuals with criticism of the club itself – something past owners arguably cultivated and exploited. Being able to make the distinction is a lesson well worth learning for future generations of fans.

It would be unfair, however, to depict Rangers fans as completely in thrall to either Sir David Murray or Craig Whyte. For example, during

---

[1] Alex Thomson, 'Piercing the wall of silence surrounding Rangers "fans"', *Channel 4 News*, 26 October 2012

the Murray era, the Rangers Supporters Trust's (RST) 'We Deserve Better' campaign sought to draw attention to various financial failings, the lack of strategic vision at boardroom level and a tendency to treat:

> Rangers fans with disdain as 'customers' instead of valuing and work-
> ing with them as 'supporters' and part of the Rangers family.[2]

It is possible to see this campaign, and documents such as *Setting the Standard*, which was produced by the *Gersnet* website, as evidence of a support that was well capable of engagement, imagination and reasonable criticism. These were two notable examples of Rangers fans trying to take responsibility for the direction of the club and there was a culture of dissent which varied in intensity throughout the stewardship of both Murray and Whyte.

Football naturally encourages nostalgia but this has been exacerbated over the past two decades by the incredible transformations witnessed in the game. There is a widespread yearning for the bygone days of yore, even among those who never experienced them first-hand. In Scotland, a once proud footballing country that now seems to collectively aspire to mediocrity, the moderate commercialisation of the game has been accompanied by a serious decline in the quality of the product fans are over-charged to watch. This is a truly lethal combination and the rows upon rows of empty seats at SPL grounds are reminiscent of tombstones. The decline in quality has naturally had a detrimental effect on the ability of our teams to compete with those from other countries; success has become the exception rather than the norm. More often than not, Europe has been the arena where our deficiencies have been cruelly exposed.

The tensions between what we think football is and was have been explored in a number of books with a Scottish dimension, such as Gary Imlach's *My Father and Other Working Class Heroes* and Daniel Gray's *Stramash*. For his book, Gray visited a number of Scotland's lower league grounds, spurred on by this disillusionment with top-flight English football. He was on a quest for the lost soul of football, something relatively untouched by what he condemned as 'existence for the sake of moneyed existence'.[3] It might be suggested that Rangers fans have been forced to

[2] Rangers Supporters Trust, 'We Deserve Better' Statement, www.rangerssup-porterstrust.co.uk/rstsite/index.php?option=com_content&view=article&id=241:we-deserve-better&catid=1&Itemid=43

[3] Daniel Gray, *Stramash: Tackling Scotland's Town and Teams* (Luath Press, 2010), p.12.

follow *en masse* in Gray's footsteps. Has football destroyed the best of itself by allowing capitalism to triumph over community? Or is it still anchored by a relationship between club and support that has been relatively unaffected? The Rangers story arguably provides some of the most compelling evidence anywhere in world football to support each of those positions. Financial insanity and administrative ineptitude wrought havoc on a Scottish institution but the response of the fans was a potent reminder that the soul of football is not irredeemably corrupted. What we are dealing with is a parable for the global game.

This chapter will have two main themes: football fandom in 21st century Scotland and the role of new forms of media. The first part will examine how Scottish football became polarised as it tried to come to terms with the Rangers crisis and all that it entailed. Unprecedented turmoil and adversity have been the catalyst for a cultural explosion within the Rangers support in the same way that the failure of the 1979 referendum on devolution and Thatcherism heralded a renaissance in Scottish culture – this will be the focus of the second part of the chapter. It will discuss the emergence of new websites and magazines such as *The Rangers Standard*, the *Copland Road Organization* and *Seventy2*, and record the fundraising achievements of the Rangers Fans Fighting Fund and the Red and Black Rangers campaign. In doing so, it will provide evidence to challenge the simplistic narrative that has posited social media on the side of those opposed to Rangers and demonstrate that it played an important role in bringing Rangers fans together and promoting ideas and schemes that originated from within the support.

The journalist and Celtic fan Kevin McKenna wrote shortly after Rangers entered administration that three groups would be pleased by such a turn of events: middle-class faux intellectuals, fans of clubs from Scotland's other major cities and Celtic fans. He went on to note that many Celtic fans he had spoken to saw the crisis as 'an opportunity for exacting a terrible cultural revenge', and he was among the first to be mindful of the tedium Celtic would be forced to endure in the absence, temporary or permanent, of their great rival. The sheer level of hostility witnessed, particularly on social media, supports McKenna's argument: the financial difficulties of a football holding company gave rise to a level of bitterness that can only be fully understood with reference to factors outwith football. McKenna was able to transcend petty tribalism and see the social and cultural anguish that the complete disintegration of Rangers would entail. He argued:

For many families in the west of Scotland's most socially deprived and disadvantaged housing estates, Rangers FC provides the glue that keeps their sense of pride and dignity intact. Society has taken away everything else in their lives; their jobs, their futures, their purpose, their health, their self-respect and their liberation.[4]

Such empathy, and sense of perspective and scale, would prove to be conspicuous by its absence in the forthcoming weeks and months.

In Scotland, the Rangers story (stories might be more accurate) became exhibit A in the battle between traditional forms of media on the one hand and blogs and social media on the other. For some, the nature of the coverage signalled the decline of print and broadcast journalism and the triumph of blogs and online content of vastly varying quality and intent. Furthermore, this clash was quite deliberately given ideological dimensions and framed in a simplistic and binary way as a clash between 'the establishment' and 'the people' and was mapped all too neatly onto events taking place in the world of Scottish football. The phrase 'Scottish Spring'[5] was used liberally and inappropriately to describe what was being portrayed as a social media enabled campaign to thwart the pro-Rangers machinations of the Scottish football authorities. This was really just a tired old cliché adorned with some tatty 21st century accessories. On the establishment side we had Rangers and the so-called 'mainstream media', on the other we had the people using social media and emboldened by the information published on investigative blogs such as *Rangers Tax Case* (RTC). Those using social media were portrayed as engaged, connected and righteous while Rangers fans were reduced to a sort of bovine dependency on the 'succulent lamb' journalism of the mainstream media.

Much of the prestige and self-importance of the coalition of blogs devoted to the Rangers situation was derived from the Orwell Prize awarded to the RTC blog. It conferred a sense of status and gave the narrative they were collectively dedicated to promoting a veneer of plausibility and, as a result, many journalists paid homage despite one of RTC's guiding principles being utter contempt for their abilities and professionalism. Another irony lay in RTC and others damning the alleged pro-Rangers

---

4 Kevin McKenna, 'Don't be too quick to gloat at the plight of Rangers', *The Observer*, 19 February 2013 (My thanks to Professor Tom Gallagher for bringing this article to my attention.)

5 Gerry Hassan, 'The Wave of Democratic Protest that Changed Scottish Football Will Change Society', *The Scotsman*, 4 August 2012

agenda of the mainstream media while being driven by a far more obvious agenda. Put simply, this amounted to little more than a wish to maximise the damage suffered by the club and the creation of a prejudicial media environment through the repetition of terms such as 'financial doping' and the insinuation or outright accusation of cheating. This was seemingly overlooked or deemed irrelevant by those who rushed to honour the investigative prowess of the site. To Rangers fans, the coalition of the willing had the journalistic credibility of a feverish tabloid.

Stuart Cosgrove, Head of Programmes at Channel 4 but better known in Scotland as a co-presenter of BBC Radio Scotland's *Off the Ball*, eagerly jumped on this bandwagon. In an article for the appropriately Orwellian-sounding *Scottish Football Monitor* blog, he explained the new dynamics in Scottish sports journalism. He declared there had been 'a fundamental change in the way we construct and receive knowledge', and, specifically referencing RTC, he argued:

> restricted documents are regularly shared online, where they can be analysed and torn apart. Those with specialist skills in such as insolvency, tax expertise or accountancy can lend their skills to a web forum and can therefore dispute official versions of events.

This all sounds desirable to a certain extent but in this case principle has been obscured by grubby reality and intent has, at best, been dismissed as unimportant.[6] Mike Small, the editor of the Scottish nationalist blog *Bella Caledonia*, explained how this process had apparently affected Scottish football:

> The good news is that the inept coterie of at the top of the game has been bypassed by ordinary fans and smaller clubs. This is what democracy looks like.

Furthermore, Small was of the opinion that the Scottish football authorities had been guilty of attempting to 'collude with Rangers'. Had it not been for:

> the resistance of a network of ordinary fans unconvinced by the governing bodies' (or the mainstream media's) account of things, the money men's perpetual short-termism would have prevailed.[7]

---

6   Stuart Cosgrove, 'Why the Beast of Armageddon Failed to Show', *The Scottish Football Monitor*, 5 November 2012

7   Mike Small, '"Rangers" starting in the lowest league is a victory for fans over an inept elite', *Comment is Free*, 16 July 2012

Such a claim seriously distorted the events and dynamics of the summer of 2012, as demonstrated elsewhere in this book (see chapter v by Chris Graham).

Small's arguments were echoed in *The Scotsman* by the political commentator Gerry Hassan who contended:

> football is the first arena in our public life where the fresh, cleansing air of democracy has shown itself. Over the summer, football fans across Scotland have come together, agitated, and organised and overturned the time-honoured stitch-up that would have kept a NewCo Rangers in the SPL.

He also talked easily of collusion.[8] In this way, the crisis that had befallen Rangers – the quintessentially British club – was packaged up and sold as a natural extension of the multiple crises that had afflicted the British state in recent years. Indeed, the political undertones of some of the commentary need to be acknowledged.

Hassan and Small, supporters of Dundee United and Hibernian respectively, in their eagerness to write something into being, fundamentally failed to come to terms with the underlying reality of the situation they were describing: any attempt at collusion that took place over the summer was for the benefit of their teams and others. Rangers wouldn't have derived any benefit from a crippled and demoralised existence in either the SPL or the First Division of the Scottish Football League and the majority of Rangers fans did not covet a place in either of those leagues. Any moves that were made to bring about such a scenario took place because SPL chairmen felt they were necessary for the integrity of the TV deal upon which so many were dependent. The 'No to NewCo' movement has since been shown to be the work of a relatively small number of people, mainly Facebook phantoms and 140-character-Twitter-bigshots. It was unsustainable because it was built on defiance. The 'Scottish Spring', it transpired, had the vitality of a pile of autumnal mulch.

While certain prominent individuals were pontificating with little justification about the people, 38,000 Rangers fans were buying season tickets. A couple of other brief examples can be used to give an impression of the numbers passionately engaged on each side of the debate. First, around 10,000 Rangers fans marched to Hampden at the end of April 2012 to protest the decision of an SFA tribunal to impose punishments which included a £160,000 fine and 12-month transfer ban

---

8   Gerry Hassan, 'The Wave of Democratic Protest that Changed Scottish Football Will Change Society', *The Scotsman*, 4 August 2012

relating mainly to disrepute charges. Around 100 people, a charitable estimate, attended a 'No to NewCo' protest at the same venue. Second, as of February 2013, Hibernian were the only club to show an increase in crowds season-on-season, all the others had recorded a loss compared to their average gate at the same time in 2012.[9] In early 2013, figures from SPL clubs started to comment on the lamentable support they were receiving from fans. A report on the Motherwell AGM, which took place in February 2013, quoted a club figure as saying:

> the club (and other SPL clubs too) had been let down by the fans who had influenced the vote over the summer with the promise of increasing attendances.

Terry Butcher, the manager of Inverness Caledonian Thistle, criticised the fans of his club after only 2,529 attended a mid-week game against Kilmarnock – this despite the Highland side being second in the league at the time. He was quoted as asking, 'Does this city deserve a football team like the one we've got just now?'[10] Like autumn leaves, fans seemed to be falling away rather than increasing in number as had been promised. It should be noted that the above is not intended to be an argument for special treatment based on the level of support the Rangers can boast. The club broke certain rules and therefore deserved to incur the penalties that were available to the football authorities. There were flawed interpretations of events, however, that paid scant regard to the many people in Scotland who were adversely affected by what was going on. With a degree of callousness, it was made clear that they were not the right people.

When news of administration was announced, the natural and laudable reaction of fans was to consider ways that they might help. The creation and success of the Rangers Fans Fighting Fund (RFFF) was one of the few unambiguously positive stories of 2012 and perhaps the most notable manifestation of this sentiment. The context was dire but the response of the fans was magnificent and, along with incredible ticket sales, the RFFF offers the most reliable testimony to the spirit that confronted adversity. Donating to the fighting fund was a way for fans to be proactive rather than having to sit back numbly while events unfolded.

---

[9] Tom English, 'Rangers verdict set to unleash hell', *The Scotsman,*
     28 February 2013

[10] Kenny Millar 'I dunno if Inverness deserves this team', *The Scottish Sun,*
     15 February 2013

Along with going to matches, it offered fans, most of whom would not have been wealthy individuals, an additional way to distil their anger and frustration into something positive. It was also a pleasant example of the club and fans working together constructively. The RFFF committee initially comprised representatives of the three main fan groups – the Rangers Supporters Trust, Supporters Assembly and Supporters Association – but also Ally McCoist, Sandy Jardine and Walter Smith, all totemic figures in the club's history. A considerable sum of money was raised in short-order and some of that money was put to good use by paying an outstanding debt of £22,000 owed to Dunfermline Athletic Football Club, a gesture that was appreciated by that club's Chairman John Yorkston. This reflected stories of individual Rangers fans taking it upon themselves to try and repay monies owed to small creditors and undermined assertions that Rangers fans had little regard for those who suffered as a result of the financial collapse of the old company.

The RFFF slipped out of the spotlight towards the end of 2012 as the situation stabilised with the start of the new season and after Charles Green's successfully orchestrated share issue, which appeared to give the club a firm financial foundation for the foreseeable future. Some matters remained to be resolved, particularly an investigation into whether football rules had been broken through the use of Employee Benefit Trusts. The new year returned the RFFF to a position of prominence after it was announced that at least some of the £538,000 in the bank at that time was to be used to employ a QC and solicitor to represent Rangers at the SPL-appointed Commission chaired by Lord Nimmo Smith and tasked with looking into the matter. A statement released on 17 January 2013 announced the RFFF would be underwriting the costs incurred protecting Rangers' 54 league titles. Quoted in the statement, a spokesman said:

> It is absolutely crucial that Rangers' titles remain untouched. But because there has been a long-running campaign in the media and within certain other clubs to punish Rangers we must do everything within our power to protect the club's proud history.[11]

Many fans, the writer included, mistakenly assumed this meant the RFFF would release funds only in the event of Lord Nimmo Smith recommending Rangers be stripped of titles. This impression was subsequently corrected in information passed to *The Rangers Standard* which made it clear that the solicitor and the QC would be fighting the Rangers corner

---

[11] This statement can be found on the Rangers Fans Fighting Fund website.

at the evidence stage. The importance of this was underlined in the resulting article which argued:

> the SPL lawyers, Harper MacLeod [sic], have been relying on the fact that nobody would be present to challenge their ridiculous assertion that Rangers have been 'cheating'.[12]

This decision demonstrated the importance to the fans of the club's history and achievements: titles are something for the fans to cherish, possibly even more so than the players responsible for winning them.

With the publication of Lord Nimmo Smith's verdict on 28 February 2013, attention will eventually turn to the fate of the remaining money. The transformation of the RFFF into an investment fund is an exciting prospect and the money might contribute to a number of good causes that will form part of the positive legacy of this period in the club's history. There has, for example, been talk of using the money to repay some of the debts of the old company. Deciding how to best use the money could become a source of conflict so it will be important to be guided by the spirit which animated the collection of the money in the first place. What is clear is that social media and the internet provide the tools to survey a large swath of opinion and if fans care about the final destination of the money then they should make the effort to have their opinions heard on the subject if and when the time comes. The committee members deserve to have some confidence when it comes to spending the money and a simple poll with numerous options might be a crude way of gauging opinion but it would be a starting point.

Red and Black Rangers was another notable fan-led fundraising initiative. Money was raised through the sale of a red and black striped scarf, the fashion accessory of choice for the average football fan. Like most good ideas, the success of the initiative was built on a foundation of simplicity and those responsible for making it a reality – Stuart MacLean, Will Craig and Jim O' Donnell – deserve a great deal of credit. The three fans were brought together by Mark Dingwall of the RST following discussions on the popular *FollowFollow* forum which he takes a leading role in. MacLean considered the backing of the RST to be vital to the eventual success of the campaign which was promoted enthusiastically using social media. The scarves were sold, with assistance from the Rangers Ticket Office and fan volunteers, for £10 with the profit of over £7.50

---

[12] Chris Graham, 'SPL Tribunal – Good News and More Questions', *The Rangers Standard*, 23 January 2013

being channelled to the club. Following advice from Administrators Duff & Phelps, it was decided that the best way to do this was by purchasing tickets which were subsequently donated to schools, children's charities, football clubs and the Boys Brigade. Around £50,000 was raised in this way with some of the money also being used to pay for 50 children to attend the Linfield-Rangers game in Belfast.

The scarves became commonplace with remarkable speed and represented an unambiguous declaration of support for the club. MacLean was particularly struck by the number of fans wearing them at the Rangers-Celtic game. The colour combination was selected for a number of reasons. The Rangers reserve or A-team, once known as The Swifts, played in red and black vertical stripes. The choice was also a nod to the colours of the burgh of Govan and the socks worn in recent times by the first team which are black with a red fold. There was also a more basic need to distinguish the scarf from the popular red, white and blue item favoured by many Rangers fans. The Govan link was emphasised by the adoption of the burgh's motto *Nihil Sine Laboure* – nothing without work. The campaign was wound down shortly after the start of the 2012–13 season and the remaining scarves were donated to the Rangers Charity Foundation.

One of the early casualties of the cost-cutting necessitated by administration was the club's *Rangers Monthly* publication. This was a relatively new venture that built on the legacy of the popular *Rangers News* magazine.[13] The absence of a quality printed magazine devoted to the club might have been a minor concern given the context but it was nevertheless encouraging to see the fans doing something to at least partially fill the gap. *Seventy2* was the second title to be launched by Media73 Ltd, which is owned by Rangers and Sunderland fans. Media73 already published *Seventy3*, a Sunderland magazine, which had been launched at the start of the 2011/12 season. James Donaldson, *Seventy2*'s editor, describes it as a retro magazine distinct from both established fanzines and the now extinct club publications. It is edited by fans and the bulk of the copy for each issue is sourced from supporters but the quality of the production distinguishes it from fanzines, such as *Follow Follow* and *Number One*, which have an endearing, do-it-yourself appearance. Another level of separation is provided by former players acting as guest editors and columnists and the magazine is already available in shops such as Asda and WH Smith.

---

[13] Colin Armstrong, 'No News is Bad News', *The Rangers Standard*, 26 July 2012

Donaldson explained how he came to be involved:

> As soon as the *Seventy2* Twitter account popped up in March 2012, I found it and got in touch to offer my services as an editor, as I had been in the role of News Editor at *Rangers Media* for 6 months and felt it was time to add to my football media experience.

He is assisted by small team which includes Creative Director/Sales Manager Andrew Brewster and editor-in-chief Mal Robinson. Donaldson, who also appears regularly on the popular *We Are The People* podcast, explained that the magazine was in the pipeline before administration. But he felt all those events perhaps gave the concept of a retro magazine, which contains a great deal of historical content, a touch more relevance. It is possible, then, to see *Seventy2* as an extension of the new found intensity with which Rangers fans protect their history. A renewed interest in the club's history was detectable prior February 2012 but this has subsequently been transformed into something more intense. Erroneous claims that Rangers are dead have stoked interest into a burning sense of ownership.

Donaldson outlined his plans for the future development of *Seventy2*. In the short term, the objective is to solidify the position of the magazine and aim for a steady increase in sales. In the medium term, the plan is to increase the exposure through a partnership with Rangers Supporters' Clubs and the major supporters' groups. Individual supporters' clubs will be given the opportunity to sell copies of the magazine in return for retaining a slice of the profit. The long term aim is more ambitious and would necessitate a more formal relationship with the club itself. Donaldson said:

> I would ideally like Rangers to sell the magazine through their usual outlets as I believe it is more than good enough to be an official affiliated product – and more fans should know about it so they can enjoy it too. Plus, if Rangers can make money, by doing nothing other than approving and selling the product, how can they lose?

The *Copland Road Organization* (CRO) was one of the most prominent websites to have emerged from the debris of 2012. The fan responsible for creating the site was Shane Nicholson, a no-holds-barred American who first came to prominence as a source of information on the US trucking tycoon Bill Miller. CRO developed out of Nicholson's contributions on *Rangers Media* and he brought experience in journalism, design and marketing to bear on the task of creating a blog that could make a considerable impact in a short period of time – an objective he achieved. In the age of the tweet and forum post, CRO's content is article based, albeit that some can be short in length. A site of this nature will inevitably prosper or wither based on the quality of its content but Nicholson, perhaps understandably, also cites the design of the site as crucial. Its red and black colour scheme is simultaneously visually striking and a nod, intentional or otherwise, to the Red and Black Rangers campaign discussed above.

Social media was instrumental, in a number of ways, in the site's success. An exchange with a *Scotland on Sunday* journalist and Motherwell director was crucial for Nicholson in terms of establishing its tone and clarifying the purpose he wanted it to fulfil. He explained:

> I took on a Motherwell board member… in a Twitter spat, the SNP's Andrew Wilson. His quote that we should hope to 'find redemption' for the sins of our club was probably the watershed moment for me in terms of realising what we were up against in Scottish football.

Nicholson added:

> Here was the director of another SPL club telling me that I as a Rangers fan should seek the cross of the football gods for the deeds of our past owners.

Nicholson gradually gathered together a group of writers and designers, notably Andy McKellar, Alan Clark, Peter Ewart, Bill McMurdo and Andy McGowan, who were ready, willing and able to take the fight to the club's detractors and occasionally those connected to it. With an informal division of labour now in place, Nicholson was free to become, in his words, 'more of a media attack dog, something which I honestly revel in'. The personality of the site, which Nicholson describes as 'snarky, facetious, sarcastic, biting, but informative and most importantly fun', owes much to his formative influence. Regular podcasts have become a popular part of CRO's output and they are characterised by sprawling anecdotes which differentiate it from the more mundane fare of sports podcasts.

The other website to have emerged recently is *The Rangers Standard*. The site's mission statement reads:

> This is an opportunity to examine the club's history and development, reclaim neglected or forgotten parts of its heritage, and reflect how the Rangers community develops from here and how the future might be shaped by the concerns, hopes and visions of committed supporters.

The site was very much born out of a belief that the crisis engulfing the club had to be used as positively as possible. It was believed that wide-ranging debate among fans could be part of the revitalisation of Rangers. It was also hoped that the site might slowly undermine some of the existing negative stereotypes used when discussing 'Rangers fans'. Similar to the *Copland Road Organization*, the focus is primarily on articles with a forum dedicated to discussing them following publication. The intent and ethos of the site attracted contributions from academics and journalists while others have praised its content. The respect for the site can be evidenced by the regular appearance of those involved, particularly Chris Graham, on radio, television and in print when a fan's perspective is required on Rangers stories. John DC Gow, furthermore, has become ESPN's foremost writer about the club.

Social media featured prominently in the development of both CRO and TRS. The impetus for each site has come from social media interaction with other fans, which has established relationships and encouraged those involved to expand to formats able to do justice to the complexities and challenges thrown up by the financial crisis. Social media sites such as Twitter were subsequently important in promoting content and cultivating a network of readers and contributors. The reach afforded by this method of promotion has seen both sites regularly receive five-figure hits for articles, some of which have drawn favourable responses from journalists working for established broadcasters and newspapers. Social media has also been shown to have played an instrumental role in the creation of *Seventy2* through the recruitment of the magazine's editor, sourcing of copy and promotion. Such evidence serves to undermine misguided notions about the role of social media in the events of the past year. It has allowed Rangers fans to grow creative ventures that reflect their passion for their club, arguably a more worthwhile use of the technology than that lauded by those who know little about what goes on amongst Rangers fans.

For those same fans, there was much to regret in the year that followed February 2012. But it was also a year in which the generations-old bond between football club and support was tested, reaffirmed and celebrated. In Scotland, however, this was routinely characterised as defiance of others rather than an expression of support for Rangers. The defiance argument implied that Rangers fans had a relationship with their club that was different from that which exists between other fans and clubs. Gordon Waddell was one journalist who admitted he had been wrong to favour this interpretation. In one of his *Sunday Mail* columns he confessed:

> the bottom line is the vast majority of their fans are simply there to support their team. They're there because it's 3pm on a Saturday and it's all they ever wanted to do.[14]

---

[14] Gordon Waddell, 'Rangers are being supported admirably... but the club is being run abysmally', *Sunday Mail*, 10 February 2013

Alan Pattullo, writing in *The Scotsman*, took a different approach and reflected one of the main arguments this chapter has sought to put forward:

> As ever, the burden created by the excessive spending – or the determined non-payment – of others has been transferred into the hands of the supporters, who have risen to the occasion. It is this spirit that deserves to be saluted today.[15]

In a sense, football was simplified for Rangers fans in 2012 and something that had long been dormant was reawakened. Suddenly, hearing the Champions League music at Ibrox every season was exposed, correctly, as a luxury as opposed to a necessity. There is one lesson that should be afforded prominence ahead of all others: clubs can only rely on their fans in their hour of need. New business models, the proliferation of corporate sponsorship and TV mega deals (Scotland need not apply) have arguably obscured this fundamental truth but Rangers fans have reiterated it for all to see. Football retains the potential to inspire people and new technology allows that inspiration to be shared, enhanced and built upon. When future generations ask who saved Rangers and revitalised the club thereafter, the fans of today can say with some confidence: 'We were the people.'

---

[15] Alan Pattullo, 'Rangers anniversary should celebrate fan spirit', *The Scotsman*, 14 February 2013

CHAPTER VIII

We Don't Do Walking Away

IAIN DUFF

IT WAS A warm, sunny August evening as we made our way to Ibrox, my dad, my seven-year-old son and me. No jackets required, as Phil Collins would say. I must have walked this route hundreds of times over the years and I could do it with my eyes closed. We turn right out of the subway station onto Copland Road, pass the programme and fanzine sellers and squeeze through the long queue outside the entirely inappropriately-named Sportsman chip shop, resisting the temptation to stop for a king rib supper or some other grease-infused delight. Briefly we stop at one of the street vendors and look for an unofficial Simpsons-themed Rangers scarf for my son. Unfortunately they don't have any, or at least none that I'm willing to let my young son wear, despite his Homer Simpson obsession. Next we pass the Ladbrokes on the corner of Copland Road and Mafeking Street, where business is booming. As we shuffle past, I remember how it had housed the Rangers Shop when I first made this journey thirty-odd years earlier. My memory is that all it sold was old match programmes and baby items emblazoned with dreadful puns (eg 'I'm the best dribbler at Ibrox' and 'I'm potty about Rangers'). It seems like a different world, yet at the same time, one so familiar.

Then comes 'The Moment'. We turn the corner into Mafeking Street and pause for a moment to take in the view. Rising above the sea of heads like a huge cruise liner sitting in harbour is Ibrox Stadium. It's a view I've seen so many times before, but that first glimpse never fails to take the breath away. Other stadiums might be newer, might stand taller, but there is no other like Ibrox. I suppose everyone feels the same way about their club's home ground, but I'm afraid they are all deluded fools. We carry on towards the megastore, pass alongside the Govan Stand and head towards the Broomloan Road end, where three seats were reserved for us in the family section.

This was a momentous occasion for us Duffs; three generations of our family off to see the Rangers together for the first time. But it was a special occasion on a wider scale too. The match in question was the opening home game of the 2012–13 season, a League Cup tie against East Fife. Nothing particularly special about that you might think, until you consider the turbulent events of the previous six months. As unthinkable as it might have seemed, this great Scottish institution had stood on the abyss – with the very real prospect that it might cease to exist. In February 2012, the company that ran Rangers had gone into administration, setting off a chain of events that would eventually see the football club forced to play in the fourth tier of Scottish football.

Of course, Rangers' downfall had been viewed with unbridled glee by fans of opposition clubs who saw it as an opportunity to settle old scores they would never be able to avenge on the pitch and urged their own clubs to swing the boot. Some clubs seemed only too eager to oblige, while others preferred to keep public comments to a minimum, despite strong suspicions that behind closed doors they were delighted at the prospect of an emasculated Rangers. Meanwhile, plenty of media commentators made it clear that they too were enjoying the demise of Scotland's biggest club, goading Rangers supporters with bizarre and illogical demands for apologies and demonstrations of contrition. Cynics also predicted (hoped?) that the 'glory hunters' whom they claimed populated the stands at Ibrox would simply walk away now that the club had been dumped into the Third Division.

But instead of abandoning ship, the fans rallied behind the club they loved. Inspired by manager Ally McCoist, legendary ex-player Sandy Jardine, and even new owner Charles Green, supporters were reinvigorated. The sudden prospect of losing something that was such a vital part of so many people's lives re-ignited smouldering passions. Crowds at the final few games of the 2011–2 season held up, while a rally at Hampden protesting against SFA punishments attracted more fans than any match in Scotland played that day. But as the new season approached there were still doubts in some quarters about how the Rangers fans would respond. As we will see, they needn't have worried.

These days I live a few hundred miles away from Glasgow and family and work commitments mean travelling to games regularly is not an option. But in fact I'd given up my fortnightly pilgrimages to Ibrox long before I moved away. The arrival of two children on the scene and the need to save money was a convenient excuse for giving up my once-cherished season ticket, but the truth was that I'd fallen out of love with football. The passion had gone. I still loved Rangers, but we were no longer *in* love.

How had it come to this? I'd been going to Ibrox since I was five years old and witnessed more than thirty years of ups and downs but had never once considered giving up. I endured the misery of the first half of the eighties under John Greig and Jock Wallace with the sort of stoicism that you rarely see in teenagers. When Dick Advocaat's expensively assembled squad imploded in the early 2000s, I trudged along every week without fail. The latter part of the Alex McLeish regime was tough going and Paul Le Guen's short but stormy time in charge stretched my patience to its very limit. Call me a glutton for punishment, but at no point during any of these depressing periods did I seriously think about quitting.

However as the first decade of the new millennium drew to a close something changed in my attitude towards football, and Rangers in particular. I was becoming increasingly disenchanted by the circus that now surrounded the Scottish game, particularly the Old Firm, and especially when the two clubs met. At some point, the actual football on the pitch had become of secondary importance to the 'controversy'.

The tipping point for me came in the aftermath of a Scottish Cup tie at Parkhead in March 2011, which Celtic won one–nil. Two Rangers players were sent-off during the game and a third – El Hadji Diouf, who'd earlier had a bizarre on-pitch argument with Celtic boss Neil Lennon – was shown a red card after the match. Meanwhile Rangers assistant manager Ally McCoist and Lennon squared up to each other on the touchline after the final whistle. But it wasn't what happened at the match that left me disillusioned. For all the flashpoints, no punches were thrown and no-one was hurt. It was an important football match – tensions were high and tempers frayed. The scenes were not particularly edifying, but you see the same thing every week at football grounds up and down the country, in fact all over the globe.

But predictably, the match was to provoke yet another outbreak of handwringing, wailing and teeth-gnashing about 'Scotland's shame'. Politicians, police and the football authorities fell over themselves to express their outrage, and of course grab a few headlines of their own with illogical and unrealistic calls for Old Firm games to be banned. This orgy of mock outrage left me utterly fed-up with the game. But in reality, it had been coming for some time. The last decade had seen more and more focus on non-footballing matters like sectarian singing and fan misbehaviour, topped off by paranoia-fuelled complaints about supposedly biased refereeing and officialdom. More than anything, I was fed-up with the tit-for-tat attempts at point-scoring that now passed for Old Firm conflict. What had once been a relatively 'normal' – if admittedly somewhat acrimonious – rivalry had turned into something poisonous, weird and at times quite obsessively creepy. Frankly, I was sick of it and wanted out.

This was no easy break-up. My love affair with Rangers had been a long one. It started in 1977 when my father took me to Ibrox for the first time to see Rangers play Dundee United. I don't remember a huge amount about the game or the day but I do vividly recall writing about it and drawing a picture in my school diary the following Monday. The drawing was of Rangers scoring what was the only goal of the game – and featured a United player with one arm in the air claiming offside. It was to become common theme over the next thirty years.

Later the same season, I went to another game against St Mirren when I got to sit on one of the wooden benches in the old Centenary Stand. Such luxury! After much badgering, I was bought a match programme and I spent a good part of the game reading about people with exotic names I'd never heard before, like McCloy, Greig and Jardine. I decided to mark the players I liked with a tick and those I didn't with a cross. Unsurprisingly the St Mirren players were all given an 'X', while all but one of the Rangers players received a tick. Poor old Peter McCloy was the sole recipient of the black mark and I've no idea to this day what he did to upset the five-year-old me. Whatever it was, it was a harsh way to treat a loyal club servant, but such are the fickle ways of the football fan.

By the early eighties I was going to Ibrox on a regular basis. The old terraces and the Centenary Stand had gone and were replaced with three gleaming new state-of-the-art stands. Unfortunately the successful team of the late seventies had also gone and was replaced with a somewhat less than gleaming collection of players. These were generally depressing times for Rangers fans but, while glory-hunting school pals suddenly started supporting Aberdeen, Dundee United and even Celtic, I stuck with it. My heroes were baby-faced striker John MacDonald and hard-as-nails club captain John McClelland, who represented Northern Ireland at the World Cup in 1982. That Scotland had precisely no Rangers players in their squad for the same competition, neatly demonstrated just how bad the club was faring at the time.

Four years later – and it felt like longer at the time – everything changed. Graeme Souness arrived as Rangers manager and blew through the club and Scottish football like a hurricane. Players like Terry Butcher, Chris Woods and Graham Roberts snubbed big English clubs to come north to Ibrox and helped Rangers win the league for the first time in nine years.

From the all-time low of being the fifth best team in Scotland, the arrival of Souness brought instant glamour to the dour Scottish game and levels of optimism not seen around Ibrox for a decade. When the title was finally won at Pittodrie in April 1987, there were outpourings of joy the likes of which haven't been witnessed since. I was 15 and had no real memory of Rangers ever winning the league, and for me, that season remains the high water mark of my time as a fan. Of course there were lots of good times to follow – the arrival of Laudrup and Gascoigne, Nine in A Row, the early Advocaat years, countless Old Firm victories and especially the road to Manchester – but none have come close to matching the sheer excitement and exhilaration of 1986-7. The first time is always the sweetest.

Fast forward a quarter of a century to 2011. A few weeks after the latest 'shame game' I moved south for work, and while I obviously enjoyed the climax of the season which resulted in a third successive title win for Walter Smith, things had definitely changed. Whereas in the past I would have sought out pubs showing Rangers games I couldn't attend on TV, I was now happy to follow the progress of matches online or even catch results on the evening news.

My mood wasn't helped by the takeover of the club in May of 2011 by Craig Whyte. Although I doubt he would have remembered me, Craig and I had history. A decade earlier, when I was chief reporter at Glasgow's *Evening Times*, he had threatened (and failed) to sue me over a series of articles I wrote about his business practices and the collapse of a number of companies he was connected with. A lot of people had lost their jobs and considerable amounts of money as a result and when his name was first linked to Rangers my heart sank. In fact I believe my exact words were: 'I don't want him anywhere near Rangers Football Club.'

What surprised and puzzled me was the fact that no newspapers or broadcasters seemed to want to dig into Whyte's past, even though the cuttings libraries were full of highly negative stories. By the time the media started to look properly at his history, the damage had already been done and Rangers were well down the path that would lead to administration.

By February 2012, when the Administrators Duff (no relation) & Phelps were appointed, I was, as we say in Scotland, scunnered. But what really shocked more than anything was the reaction from fans of other clubs – or at least those with the platform to shout loudly about it. As Rangers suffered one ignominy after another – points deductions, expulsion from the SPL, a ban from Europe, the departure of most of the first team squad and a signing embargo – the gloating from these opposition fans grew to frenzied levels. Preposterously, many seemed happy for their own clubs to suffer as long as Rangers were seen to be punished. The buzz phrase of the summer was 'sporting integrity', yet no-one could really explain what it meant... beyond 'sticking it up the Huns'.

This was an attitude you would perhaps expect from Celtic fans, but not necessarily from supporters of other clubs. It was an indication of just how much things had changed. In years gone by, Rangers were considered to be 'Scotland's club' – the one every football fan had as their second team. Scotland forward Denis Law summed it up in an article that appeared in a Rangers supporters' annual in the early sixties. 'As a boy, like nearly everyone else in Aberdeen, I'd go to watch the Rangers,' he recalled. Expanding on this, he said:

> A visit from the mighty men of Ibrox is something special in any town – a gala day. No matter what your 'first claim' club may be, Rangers will always have a particular place in your heart if you are a Scot, because the club represents all that is best in Scottish football.

Even if the gist of Law's comments still held true, which sadly it doesn't, it's hard to imagine a modern day player daring to say it. It would mean instant demonisation. Football fans' attitudes in general have changed over the years, becoming far more tribal than in the past, so it's perhaps inevitable that sympathy for Rangers' plight would be in short supply. But the sheer vitriol took most Rangers supporters by surprise. Right now the natural inclination of Rangers fans is to metaphorically stick two fingers up at those who put the boot in, and while that's understandable, the truth is the club needs allies on its journey back to the top, so this bad feeling is an issue that needs to be addressed at some point in the near future.

The combination of being kicked from pillar to post on a daily basis and the very real prospect that the club might simply cease to exist had a strange effect on Rangers fans. Instead of giving up and turning their back on the club, they rallied behind figureheads like Ally McCoist and Sandy Jardine. Days after administration, McCoist delivered what would become a famous line: 'This is my club', he said, 'the same as it is for thousands and thousands of Rangers supporters, and we don't do walking away.'[1]

Indeed they don't, as would be proved time and time again when the new season got underway. The fans' passion was suddenly reignited. However Peter Ewart, a member of the Lothian True Blues supporters' club, recalls how there was an initial reluctance from supporters to commit to buying season tickets because of the uncertainty over the club's ownership and future direction:

---

[1]   Pete O'Rourke, 'McCoist committed to Gers', Sky Sports website, www. skysports.com/football/news/11788/7525877/McCoist-committed-to-Gers, 17 February 2012

The press had reported only 250 renewals by the first week in July. It was clear that of our supporters club, only a few had renewed by mid-July. There was a lot of debate about why you would or wouldn't have renewed. Many were playing the wait and see game, myself included. Our club president, Ricky, gave us some food for thought, though. I asked why he had renewed with so much uncertainty. The answer was brilliant. It was along these lines 'I figured that Rangers would be playing somebody next season, and that I'd be going to see them, so I renewed.' Asked what if he lost his money. 'If I lose my money then we'll have bigger things to worry about.' You can't argue with any of that!

It took a concerted effort by Charles Green to persuade fans that he could be trusted, helped in no small part by a direct appeal from McCoist. With his blessing, the supporters responded. Despite being consigned to play in the Third Division of the SFL, supporters queued for hours in their thousands to renew season tickets. The total number sold eventually exceeded 38,000 and was actually higher than the previous season in the SPL. Average attendances in the Third Division were only bettered in the British Isles by Manchester United, Arsenal and Newcastle United.

But it wasn't just about the numbers, as important as they were. There was a real feel-good factor at play, a sense of adventure and excitement that had been missing for so long in the mundane, repetitive slog of the SPL. And that brings us back to that sunny evening in August. As the three of us walked round to the Broomloan stand, we encountered huge queues of fans at each turnstile. So large were the crowds that the kick-off had to be delayed to let everyone in. The buzz of anticipation outside the ground translated to an electric atmosphere when the game finally got under way.

The scenes that night and the images of fans queuing for season tickets transported me back to 1986 when there were similar scenes at Ibrox every week. In the days before season tickets became the norm, tickets had to be bought for each match. And every week, without fail, thousands of supporters would queue up, whatever the weather, to ensure they had a seat for the next match. It was dramatically different circumstances, but the same positive feeling that surrounded the club in the first season under Souness appeared to have returned to Ibrox. Not only that, but there was a unity in the support that had been missing in recent years. As Peter Ewart explains, this came as a surprise to many:

> It is clear that some outside Rangers completely underestimated the strength of bond that exists between the club and the fans and between the fans themselves. Rangers is our club – nothing had changed in that respect and that was massively reassuring.

This new unity was something that Charles Green had done well to tap in to. His criticisms of the football authorities and the players who walked out on the club had created something of a siege mentality that drew the fans closer together and probably helped shift a few more season tickets.

Not everyone was happy at the feel-good factor in the Southside of Glasgow, though. The Rangers fans' positive response infuriated those whose ambition was to see the club die. Rival fans reacted like a jealous ex, who can't come to terms with the fact that the person they dumped has moved on and is now happier than ever. And needless to say, the same pundits who'd predicted apathy and empty stands were predictably contemptuous, sneeringly dismissing the response of the Rangers fans as 'defiance'.

It's easy to reject this simplistic analysis out of hand, but is there any truth in it? Were Rangers fans really turning out in huge numbers as some sort of bloody-minded, point-scoring exercise? Well to be fair, there probably *was* an element of that and it's hardly surprising, given what they had gone through over the previous six months. But to suggest this was *the* motivating factor – or even a particularly significant one – does the fans a disservice and is frankly insulting.

Speaking for myself, I know that when I decided to travel up for that League Cup game against East Fife, defiance did not enter my mind for a moment. I'd seen the club I'd followed through thick and thin for 30 years come perilously close to disappearing and I wanted to be there when they returned to action. Not to send some sort of 'get it up you' message to the rest of Scottish football, but because I had been reminded of what football was all about – the unity, the shared memories, the pride in your club and the people that represent it. After all that had happened, when Rangers made their first appearance of the season at Ibrox, I wanted to be there to share that experience with my fellow fans, to tell the players, coaches and everyone else at the club that I hadn't abandoned them and to thank *them* for not walking away.

For me it was refreshing to be able to enjoy the positive things about football and to take a break from the politics that had been suffocating the game. Of course, it wasn't long before the bitterness returned, but it was fun while it lasted. And fun was the key element. Every away game saw Rangers visit (and pack out) grounds that they had rarely played at before, if at all. After the repetitious monotony of the SPL, there was a freshness about it all that made the experience more enjoyable, even if it was a little uncomfortable at times.

It was assumed by many that the novelty factor of the SFL would wear off quickly for Rangers supporters but to their credit they continued to turn out in huge numbers throughout the season, both at home and away, even when the football wasn't quite up to the standard they were used to. The question now will be whether this first season was a one-off or whether the interest will be sustained in the future.

The quality of football might be an issue, with discontent bubbling under the surface throughout the 2012–3 season, despite the convincing title win. Ally McCoist may have been a hero on the pitch and he was a magnificent leader when the club's very future was in the balance, but neither of those facts spared him from harsh criticism over some of the performances under his management. The prospect of another season of mediocre play might discourage some fans from investing in season tickets again.

Whatever the future might hold, it is undoubtedly the case that the fans have demonstrated levels of loyalty and commitment that even their harshest critics would have to acknowledge. The events of 2012 were a nightmare but some good did come of them. They reminded us that Rangers Football Club was something worth caring about and something worth fighting for. For some of us, that reminder was badly needed. My biggest hope is that it will never be required again.

CHAPTER IX

Behind the Convenient Myth of Sporting Integrity

GAIL RICHARDSON

I BEGIN THIS chapter with an assertion which probably colours every-thing that follows it: under no circumstances would I hurt the club I love in order to hurt yours. It's a truth I thought would be universally appli-cable to football fans everywhere but, as events within Scottish football in 2012 demonstrated, this is not the case.

When the company running Rangers Football Club entered adminis-tration on 14 February 2012, I was sad but not shocked. We knew it was coming, no matter how hard we wished it wasn't. Rumours had been circulating and it was clear that something was far from well within the club. I hope that in time, a full and honest account of how Rangers passed into the hands of Craig Whyte will come to light but, for now, what is known is that he purchased Rangers for £1 and secretly borrowed against future season ticket income to pay off the outstanding debt to Lloyds Banking Group. He also very quickly stopped paying PAYE and National Insurance on employees' wages. Craig Whyte, it sometimes seemed, deliberately drove the club to financial ruin. The reasons he did it are pretty irrelevant; Rangers were left in administration and desper-ately looking for a buyer.

Scottish football had experience of clubs in administration but, for some reason, it did not seem to have contemplated what might happen if a club was unable to come out of administration. What had just hap-pened at Rangers seemed to leave both the SFA and SPL in a state of con-fusion over how to deal with the situation. There were no existing rules to apply. It was decided that OldCo Rangers was no longer able to use its membership share in the SPL and that the existing teams would vote on whether or not the share could transfer to the NewCo. And thus was born the 'No to NewCo' movement.

Fans of a variety of clubs became very vocal online pushing the 'No to NewCo' message. The same vocal fans lobbied their club chairmen with the message that if their club voted to allow Rangers to transfer their share and remain in the SPL, they would vote with their feet and not renew season tickets. The SPL clubs were faced with a difficult situation and some of them dealt with it well, trying to balance the wishes of their fans with their responsibility for the on-going financial stability of their own club. In the end, the vote on transferring the membership share was 10–1 against. Rangers were the only vote for and Kilmarnock abstained.

I can understand the views of many of the fans of other SPL clubs who believed that Rangers should not be allowed to continue in the SPL. I have spoken to some of them and the overriding view is that if it had happened to a smaller club then there would have been much less furore and there would not even have been the same level of debate. I am not sure I agree with this argument. I think a lot of debate and prevarication arose because the SFA did not have provisions for such a situation on the statutes and were essentially flying by the seat of their pants. If there had been transparent rules which everyone was aware of and could have been applied then a lot of the ill-feeling would have been avoided.

The ambiguity of the situation only worsened after the SPL clubs voted against the SPL membership transfer. Stewart Regan tried to force the SFL clubs into voting to allow Rangers into the First Division with the threat of financial calamity and a league reconstruction proposal which would be not have been advantageous to the SFL. This was an absurd situation and one that had no support amongst Rangers fans. It was this action which truly exposed the sporting integrity argument for a farce. The SFA and the SPL clubs wanted to be seen to punish Rangers but did not actually want them out of the SPL for three years, as this would have a knock-on effect on crowds and the TV deals which could be negotiated.

On 13 July the SFL clubs voted to admit Rangers to the Third Division. In response to this vote, Stewart Gilmour, chairman of St Mirren, exposed a degree of hypocrisy when he blamed the SFL clubs for the damage which would be inflicted on Scottish football. He said, 'This is horrific news for St Mirren Football Club. The consequences are terrible – catastrophic even.' He praised elements of Regan's handling of the situation and placed the blame squarely on the SFL clubs:

> Unfortunately, the people in the SFL have not bought into that [Regan's document outlining plans for Rangers in Division One]. I just hope they realise the damage they have done to Scottish football.[1]

---

[1] 'St Mirren chairman blasts 'catastrophic' vote to send Rangers NewCo to SFL3', STV website, sport.stv.tv/football/clubs/st-mirren/110905-st-mirren-boss-blasts-catastrophic-vote-to-send-rangers-to-division-3/, 14 July 2012

I can't think of a single set of events which more adequately shows the sporting integrity argument for the straw man it was. Mr Gilmour was happy to pontificate on the need for sporting integrity and punishment for Rangers but expected the SFL chairmen to swallow their integrity and do what was best for the SPL clubs.

Throughout this period many fans of SPL clubs were extremely vocal about the need to punish Rangers for their perceived sins. Many of them voted in polls, lobbied their clubs and organised campaigns such as the 'No to NewCo' movement which was extremely vocal online but could only attract a pitiful number of people to a rally at Hampden. It is clear now that it was only a minority who felt so strongly about the issue and pushed chairmen to make decisions which would create financial hardship for their clubs. At the time, several club chairmen stated that, without Rangers in the SPL, there would be a financial cost which could only be countered by rising attendances.

I was taken aback by the vehemence and the tone of much of the debate around the Rangers issue, both from fans of other clubs and the media. Rangers are far from the first club to experience financial problems. In England, both Leeds and Portsmouth have, in recent times, suffered their own issues and I spoke to fans of both teams to try to get an idea of the level of debate and antagonism there was, and is, towards their clubs.

Portsmouth entered administration for the first time in February 2010 and the resulting nine point penalty ensured they were relegated to the Championship at the end of the 2009–10 season. In June 2010 they agreed a CVA which HMRC appealed against. They came perilously close to liquidation but managed to come out of administration in October 2010. To say they have had a series of dubious owners is an understatement in my opinion, and the club has changed hands several times to people who were arguably not fit and proper to run a football club. Portsmouth entered administration again in February 2012, three days after Rangers, and received a ten point deduction. They were relegated to League One at the end of season 2011–12 and started the new season on minus ten points as a consequence of failing to come out of administration. Currently, Portsmouth Supporters Trust is attempting to buy the club and have an agreement to do so. I'm sure all football supporters empathise with them and wish them well in their quest.

I spoke to some Portsmouth supporters to gauge the reactions from other fans. In general the reaction they have experienced has been mixed. They have had jokes and jibes, in particular from Southampton fans who are their biggest rivals. There is a perception that Southampton fans would relish Portsmouth going out of business. From other fans they have received a mix of banter, support and sympathy. They have also received support from many fans of clubs where there are fan ownership schemes such as AFC Wimbledon, Swansea and Wrexham.

There is a very strong feeling that the FA has badly let the club down as the 'Fit and Proper Person' test has failed Portsmouth four times in the past five years and it would appear that the club and its fans are paying the price for that. I expect the latter part of that sentence will resonate strongly with Rangers fans. The Portsmouth Supporters Trust has received messages of support from numerous supporters' trusts, fans' groups and individuals including fans of their biggest rivals, Southampton. They have received expressions of support from Rangers and other Scottish clubs. In contrast, the Rangers Supporters Trust has received emails and messages from Portsmouth, other English clubs and football fans from as far afield as Brazil, Uruguay, Canada and Europe but not one single word from another Scottish club.

The situation at Leeds is perhaps the closest to what has happened at Rangers. After a period in administration and a failed attempt to come out of administration without a CVA, the assets of the club were sold to a NewCo and the OldCo was left to be liquidated. The Football League voted to transfer Leeds' share but imposed a penalty of 15 points. While Leeds fans felt at the time this was unfair, there is a realisation that the behaviour of Ken Bates had not been helpful and now, with hindsight, feel this was probably a fair penalty. I spoke to a Leeds season ticket holder who is also a Rangers fan and he feels that the reactions to the two situations were very different. There was no clamour for the FA to impose a harsher penalty and no campaign against Leeds keeping their league place. This Leeds fan has never had anyone suggest that Leeds are a different club or that their history has been wiped out.

It is possible that the relatively low use of social media at that time meant that the situation was not heated to the same level but, even allowing for that, it seems to be a dramatically different situation to what happened in Scotland in 2012. So what are the reasons for that difference? Why did Rangers going into administration and eventually transferring the club to a new parent company cause such animosity and strident views? I mentioned earlier in this chapter that I felt the sporting integrity argument didn't hold water but what are the real reasons?

Rangers are Scotland's most successful club and I'd be surprised if all fans of other clubs liked us. For some people there is a general mistrust or dislike of a large successful team which has been beating their team for

years and has bought their best players. In some people's eyes, Rangers are
the big boys who spent too much money and got what was coming to them.
Sir David Murray, for much of his tenure, was a strong personality and
I can imagine that many people found him arrogant and dismissive of the
rest of Scottish football. If you make statements such as 'for every five
pounds Celtic spend, we will spend ten', as Murray did in 1998, then you
have to expect a degree of *schadenfreude* when the wolves eventually
arrive at the door.

Linked to the previous point is the inherent inequality in the voting
structures of the SPL whereby many of the most important decisions require
an 11–1 majority. When Rangers were part of the SPL it meant that
Rangers and Celtic voting together ensured that any moves to alter the
distribution of wealth or the voting system floundered. Some chairmen
of the other clubs have been strong opponents of the voting system and
have lobbied hard for change. Surprisingly, in October 2012 at an SPL
board meeting, Aberdeen voted with Celtic against a motion that would
require all votes to have a 9–3 majority in order to be carried.

Popular wisdom suggests that Aberdeen were cautious about changing
the voting structure as they are opposed to any enlargement of the SPL
but, recognising that it may happen anyway, wanted to ensure they kept
a decisive say in the allocation of prize money in case they end up playing
in a league of 14 or 16.

On 11 April 2013, Stewart Milne, Chairman of Aberdeen, criticised
St Mirren for saying they were opposed to league reconstruction plans
of 12–12–18 and planned to vote against them. The irony is, of course,
that St Mirren would be unable to block the reconstruction plans if
Aberdeen had not chosen to vote against the changes to the SPL voting
structures. Regardless of this, there is a perception among many fans of
Scottish clubs that the voting system is inherently unfair and it is easy to
see how that perception has arisen and why it remains.

The *Rangers Tax Case* (RTC) website was set up by an anonymous
blogger to catalogue the details of HMRC's case against Rangers regarding their use of Employee Benefits Trusts which formed the subject of
the First Tier Tax Tribunal. It also dealt with many aspects of the change
in ownership between Sir David Murray and Craig Whyte and conse-
quently with Whyte's disastrous stewardship of the club. Several of the
revelations about Whyte's underhanded and possibly criminal dealings were
broken by this website. It undoubtedly had some very good sources,
however it is also clear that some of the documents it referred to in its
revelations should not have been in the public domain.

The *Rangers Tax Case* blog won the prestigious Orwell Prize in 2012, with the judges extolling its virtues. The problem with this of course, is that their faith in RTC was misplaced and ill-founded given that HMRC lost the First Tier Tax Tribunal. The outlandish sums of money Rangers allegedly owed to HMRC did not, after all, come to pass. HMRC have leave to appeal to the Upper Tax Tribunal and it may be as long as another year before the final verdict is handed down. No matter, the tax case blog did its job. And it did it in more ways than one. Yes, it uncovered many aspects of Craig Whyte's dealings but it also kept a steady stream of messages about Rangers' supposed giant debt in the public domain. The mainstream media was accused of being beaten to the story by RTC which was very much the case initially, but it later appeared as if some journalists were using it as a source and presenting its information as facts, rather than the opinions of an anonymous blogger.

A prime example of the internet blogger seeking to present his own agenda dressed up as 'investigative journalism' is Phil Mac Giolla Bhain. The self-styled 'rebel journalist' has a blog dealing with 'the stories that have been central to the Celtic family'. Sadly but predictably, what seems overwhelmingly central to the Celtic family are stories about Rangers.

So interested is Mac Giolla Bhain in Rangers, that he wrote a book about the club. He also persuaded *Channel 4 News'* Alex Thomson to write a foreword to the book and almost managed to get *The Sun* to agree to serialise it. It was all going so well for him until the truth came out.

Rangers fans were, rightly, incensed that a man who has spent so much time and effort denigrating them and the club was going to be lent an air of credibility by a national newspaper. Many fans, myself included, contacted the editor of *The Sun* to make them aware of Mac Giolla Bhain's previous work. This is a man who, in a clear attempt to dehumanise, refers to Rangers fans as the 'Ibrox Klan', as having a 'herrenvolk swagger'[2] and, in an interview, crassly and ludicrously compared modern day Glasgow to the Deep South of the United States in the '40s and '50s by making reference to people '[sitting] at the back of the bus'.[3]

Unsurprisingly, once the extent of Mac Giolla Bhain's hatred for Rangers became clear *The Sun* withdrew serialisation of the book immediately. In a statement explaining their decision they asserted that:

---

[2] http://www.philmacgiollabhain.ie/sevco-and-identity-theft/

[3] http://www.vavel.com/en/football/scottish-premier-league/190321-phil-mac-giolla-bhain-rangers-fans-were-persistently-mis-informed-by-their-club-and-by-the-media-who-did-not-look-too-hard-into-the-story.html

the author — previously unbeknown to us — is tarred with a sickening sectarian brush.

We believed Phil Mac Giolla Bhain to be a proper and sound journalist. *Channel 4 News* correspondent Alex Thomson obviously agreed and wrote the foreword to the book.

He was wrong and so were we.

Another keen blogger on Rangers is Paul McConville in his *Random Thoughts Re Scots Law* blog. Once again, it is surprising how many of McConville's 'random thoughts' are about Rangers. I would also be very reluctant to set too much store in his thoughts on points of law given that he is only able to practice under supervision and with the approval of the Law Society after he was found:

> guilty of Professional Misconduct in respect of his failure or unconscionable delay in replying to the reasonable enquiries of the Law Society and complying with Notices served on him by the Law Society in respect of numerous clients, his failure to reply to fellow solicitors, his failure or delay in implementing mandates, his failure to respond to clients, his failure to account timeously to clients, his failure to progress a claim on behalf of a client and his failure to honour a cheque drawn on his client account[4]

This relates to his handling of claims on behalf of dead or injured miners against the Government's Coal Liabilities Unit, which left claimants without compensation.

Now obviously both Phil Mac Giolla Bhain and Paul McConville are free to write about whatever they wish but they are not, by any stretch of the imagination, neutral observers. They write about Rangers specifically for an audience who don't like Rangers. It seems clear that they set about getting as negative a view of Rangers as possible, to as wide an audience as possible. And again, they are free to do so, but let's all be clear about what they are doing and what they hope to achieve.

At times, the tabloid coverage of the Rangers story has been nothing short of deplorable. There were occasions when hyperbole and wild guesses were all that was holding articles together. This can be the nature of the tabloid press and, as always, the choice is there not to read it but the issue is that it fuels an already inflamed situation. Twitter, Facebook and online message boards all raged during the past year. Wild speculation was presented as fact again and again. On 6 April 2012, the *Daily Record*, for example, reported that Craig Whyte had left a '£140m debt mountain'

---

4   http://www.ssdt.org.uk/findings/finding_item.asp?LTfindingID=524

at Rangers. That information entered into the public domain and was repeated until it came to be seen as fact. Rangers did not ever owe £140m but this figure persists in being mentioned to this very day.

Many journalists lined up to take a kick at Rangers. I don't subscribe in any way, shape or form to the idea of a media conspiracy but there are without doubt, individual journalists who do not like Rangers and use their profession and status to present the club in as negative a light as possible. Graham Spiers, Scottish journalist at large, was happy to label Rangers as cheats on Twitter, something he later denied. It is naïve to think that when a journalist makes this sort of comment on a public forum such as Twitter and those tweets are retweeted many times that the message isn't being spread. This clearly shows how Spiers views the situation. To think that doesn't colour what he writes would be patently ridiculous.

As part of the football licence negotiations, Rangers were asked to accept stripping of league titles and cup wins related to the on-going investigation into their use of EBTs by Lord Nimmo Smith and his panel. Despite no guilt being proven and indeed the investigation being in the early stages, pressure was brought to bear on Charles Green to accept the title stripping on behalf of Rangers

The reason this is such a vital aspect of the whole situation is that it presumes guilt and when the governing body of the game is willing to do this, it will undoubtedly have a knock-on effect on public perception. This is not the only thing which the SFA has done to inflame the situation and alter public perception. When the SFA found Rangers guilty on the disrepute charge[5] they handed down a judgement which concluded that 'only match fixing in various forms might be a more serious breach.' To even mention match fixing, generally regarded as the worst of all crimes within football, in this situation was inflammatory. It was a ridiculous parallel but one which was arguably used to alter public perception of the seriousness of the crimes Rangers were accused and prematurely found guilty of in this situation.

To suggest that examples like the ones highlighted above – Graham Spiers and the SFA using the word 'cheating', journalists talking about Rangers 'deserving' to be punished and the oft repeated £140m debt – didn't seep into the public consciousness is simply beyond belief. I have had several people tell me that Rangers were cheating long before liquidation

---

[5] For going into administration; for failing to disclose that Craig Whyte was barred from acting as a director and for failing to ensure that Craig Whyte had acted within the rules concerning fit and proper officials.

of the OldCo became an option. The reasons range from running up debt (clearly a huge amount of football clubs are currently cheating) to operating the EBT scheme. It always bears repeating that EBT schemes were perfectly legal at the time Rangers used them and that the club's dispute with HMRC was around technical aspects of how the trusts were administered.

Many people conflate the entirely separate issues of the tax on EBTs with the deliberate non-payment of PAYE and National Insurance by Craig Whyte resulting in a flimsy catch-all accusation of 'you haven't been paying your tax for years'. As I stated earlier in this chapter, I understand that people don't like Rangers but it is extremely important to acknowledge that this is a factor in many people's wish to see adequate punishment. To deny the level of dislike and even hatred that exists is sheer folly.

Some fans (mainly Celtic fans, but others too) now refer to Rangers as 'Sevco'. Despite the SFA, UEFA, the European Club Association and Lord Nimmo Smith clearly concluding that the club carried on as an entity regardless of the change in ownership, they persist in the charade that Rangers do not exist and has been replaced by something called 'Sevco' (the name of the original holding company Charles Green set up to transfer the assets of OldCo Rangers). Some of this is mischief-making and merely fans trying to wind each other up. But we are now one year on from Rangers going into administration and there are approximately 50 tweets an hour, every hour, on Twitter which include the word 'Sevco'. When Sky Sports tweeted to advertise Queens Park v Rangers as the oldest derby, it took less than a minute before they received a tweet telling them that Rangers didn't exist. They were then inundated with similar tweets. When Rangers published a prospectus for their recent Initial Public Offering (IPO) to the stock market it spoke about Rangers' 140 years of history. The regulators received complaints from rival fans claiming the prospectus was inaccurate as Rangers are a new club.

Sadly, this was not an isolated incident. On 28 March *Celtic Quick News* website reported that the Advertising Standards Authority had written to complainants to say that it was investigating claims regarding a recent Rangers advertising campaign promoting the club as Scotland's most successful football club. Reports suggest 78 people made complaints. I'm sure you find it as difficult as I do to believe that 78 grown adults, independently contacted ASA to make a complaint. It is worth pointing out that ASA are duty bound to register and investigate any such complaints. Perhaps it was the same people who contacted the stock market regulators to complain about the prospectus or the same ones who ring

STV to complain every time a Rangers supporter appears on *Scotland Tonight* to talk about Rangers. It doesn't seem too far-fetched to assume it is the same group of fans complaining to anyone who will listen, does it?

Sometimes it can seem that all perspective has been lost on this matter. To illustrate this point I'd like to tell you about my friend. I'll call him RB. RB and I have been friends for 25 years. The first inkling I had that he had taken a strong interest in the Rangers case was when we were in the pub with a group of friends shortly before Rangers went into administration. It became clear that he had spent a lot of time on the *Rangers Tax Case* website and was quoting information he had found on there as fact. I didn't pay much attention to it until he posted a message on my Facebook page four days after Rangers went into administration which said 'relegate them to the Third Division and strip them of the titles/ cups they cheated'.

Around this time he created a Twitter account which he used to tweet me messages pointing out what he thought should happen to Rangers, how we were cheats and how I was avoiding the issues by refusing to discuss them with him. I would have kept the tweets to show his lack of perspective on the issue but he deleted them within 24 hours of sending them, a pattern he continues on Twitter to this day. Towards the end of April, during a night out in the pub, things got a bit heated. Despite my protests that I didn't want to discuss it and that none of the others wanted to hear his opinions on the situation, he managed to come up with the following gems:

1   Duff & Phelps can access the Rangers Fans Fighting Fund and use it for whatever they want.

He had apparently read this online. Despite the fact that I had contributed to the RFFF and was well aware that any withdrawals from the fund had to be granted by its trustees, he was unwilling to accept my points.

2   Melt down the trophies and put padlocks on the gates of Ibrox.

At this point, and indeed even much later on in the year, there was genuine uncertainty about the future of Rangers. There were times when I doubted whether Rangers would play football in season 2012/13 and to have a friend laughingly predict the demise of the club you support is a pretty sore blow.

3   You have been cheating for years.

This referred to the case discussed earlier. Despite the verdict being months away, he was willing to state that we should be stripped of all titles and trophies won during that time and all our results should be changed to a three–nil victory to our opponents.

I would like to be able to tell you that this was banter but it wasn't. He was genuinely utterly caught up in the story and by his own admission in February 2013 'I went a bit over the top'. In the interests of fairness, I should point out here that RB is a sane, rational person – until it comes to Rangers. Thankfully our friendship endured the most difficult months of last spring and summer and we met recently to talk about things. I wanted to get to the bottom of why he felt so strongly that when I asked him if he would be happy for Rangers to go out of business even if it meant his own team would go out of business too, his answer was a resounding 'yes'.

To help me understand his feelings he had drawn me a diagram which he called 'The Wheel of Extreme Dislike'. I have replicated the diagram below for your information/amusement. Some of the points I understand, some I don't, some I would argue are merely representative of the universal resentments felt by someone who supports a 'small club' towards a bigger, more successful club and some I don't believe are true at all. It doesn't really matter, it is his perception and to him it is reality.

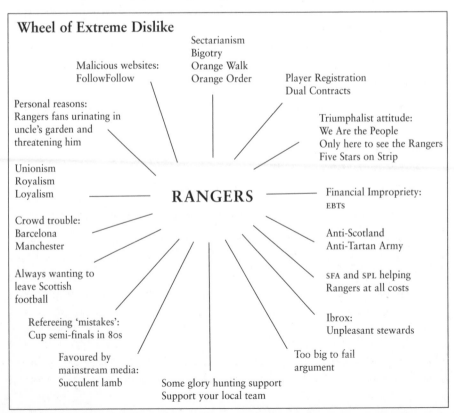

For me, it merely proved what I had been saying all along. His take on the situation and the arguments he made about Rangers needing to be punished adequately were fuelled by his dislike of the club rather than sporting principles. This is a very important point, and essentially the heart of the matter. I don't expect everyone to like Rangers and wish us well. That is a ludicrous notion. I would, however, like to see some acknowledgement of the fact that much of the anti-Rangers rhetoric which we have seen in the last year comes from a place of dislike rather than being some sort of moral standpoint.

As recently as February 2013, Tom English wrote a short article in *The Scotsman* which contained the words 'humiliation' and 'disgrace' in reference to Rangers.[6] Unlike Tom, I don't think there is any shame attached to being a Rangers fan. The support didn't cause the situation and when it happened they responded with strength and loyalty. The Rangers Fans Fighting Fund was set up and contributed to by fans in order to pay many small businesses which had been left out of pocket. Some small business owners reported that individual Rangers fans turned up with cash to pay a debt owed by the club.

Like so many Rangers fans I know, I wish this hadn't happened to my club but I refuse to feel ashamed. I would take no satisfaction in another club going through the same situation as Rangers. We are all at the mercy of owners unless we are lucky enough to be part of a fan-owned club. Even a benign owner is no guarantee of future stability. Who can guarantee the long term interest of an Abramovich or a Sheikh Mansour? At a time when supporters are pushed further and further to the margins of a game which seems increasingly beholden to the whims of TV companies, is it not time to put aside partisan considerations and appreciate that our only real allies are the fans of teams facing the same uncertainty, fear and onerous financial considerations as ourselves?

I don't seek to take rivalry out of the game, it's part of the lifeblood; but how can you look at Leeds fans, Portsmouth fans and yes, even Rangers fans and not think 'there but for fortune go I'? Maybe if we can see the things which unite us more than the things that oppose us, then there is hope for change.

---

6 Tom English, 'Rangers spin can't take away the disgrace', *The Scotsman*, 14 February 2013

CHAPTER X

The Perfect Storm

JOHN DC GOW

THERE IS LITTLE doubt that most Scottish football fans and possibly most of society took great pleasure in watching Rangers' financial demise in 2012. Some delighted in watching the big guy fall after years of being second best, while others took full opportunity of the power vacuum within the game. This might explain some of the vitriol but it cannot account for it all. It might be expected from Celtic fans but why would Dunfermline, Dundee or Greenock Morton fans become obsessed with the Rangers story and want the club to cease? Why was there so little support from politicians or others in positions of influence which would be expected when a Scottish business is in trouble and jobs could be lost? Even administration and company liquidation couldn't get much of a reaction from the Scottish Football Association, never mind open support. Unless you were a Rangers fan it seemed you wanted the club buried or were callously indifferent.

It wasn't just jealousy or opportunism, there was something more. Rangers were hated. They had become a symbol for something other than a football club and, like it or not, that symbol was sectarianism. If there was a news story about the subject then Ibrox would usually be the location. If someone wanted to gain plaudits for fighting 'Scotland's secret shame' then Rangers fans would usually be pilloried. No discussion was complete without mentioning the club, and more often than not, using the supporters as a lead example in proving bigotry exists and showing where it resides. It was this negative stereotype that enabled non-Rangers fans and the media to discuss Rangers' financial plight in grandiose moral terms. The underlying anger and disgust wasn't about finance or football, and journalist Graham Spiers pointed this out when he said:

> All over Scotland I see people dancing on Rangers' grave. It is almost like a great cultural revenge for the varied sins of this club.[1]

If the club and fans were immoral and unethical then why shouldn't society hate them – isn't that what 'good' people do? If you have some

---

[1]   twitter.com/GrahamSpiers/status/169760330333949952

politicians, people in the media and anti-sectarian charities directly or indirectly laying the blame of sectarianism at the door of Ibrox, then why wouldn't non-Rangers people want to hinder the bad guy or laugh as they fell?

Interestingly though, sectarianism is often assumed by the public to be easily defined by academics and the authorities when it is not. Most people are unaware they only hold a personal definition which tends to justify or protect their 'group', while coincidentally condemning the 'other'. Informally it becomes 'what I like' versus 'what I don't like'. For those looking for more formal definitions, one of the most widely held views in Scotland is that sectarianism concerns religious conflict between Roman Catholics and Protestants (which of course is 'fought' on the football field). As former First Minister Jack McConnell said in 2002:

> [...] Scotland will no longer tolerate acts of religious hatred. We will act to toughen the law so that courts can more severely punish crimes motivated by sectarianism.[...] It is time for the decent majority of Scots to stand up and be counted and to say that religious hatred should be put in the dustbin of history. It is time for Scotland's secret shame to be put in the past.[2]

The Catholic Church often goes further to point out that the 'problem is not so much sectarianism but anti-Catholicism.'[3] Religious sectarianism is supposedly everywhere and anyone who challenges it is at 'risk of stepping outside of the "correct" camp and of being labelled a bigot'.[4]

There is no doubt that religious sectarianism exists, nor is there much doubt that *some* Rangers fans are anti-Catholic bigots, but the extent of the problem at Ibrox and nationwide is exaggerated. Today, Rangers is a completely inclusive organisation and the vast majority of the fan-base is appalled at sectarianism (or anti-Catholicism if you wish). If they go home to Catholic wives, husbands, partners, family and friends there is no question of the remotest sectarian conflict. Even that is overstating it since few believe there is a separation to have any conflict over.

If we take footballers who are especially loved by the Rangers support we can see that the anti-Catholic stereotypes are simply not true for the majority. In a contest among the fans to determine who they would want to represent the 'best of Rangers' between Northern Irish Protestants Kyle

2   'Scotland clamps down on Sectarianism', *The Guardian,* 5 December 2002

3   Ian Dunn, 'Face up to anti-Catholicism', *Scottish Catholic Observer,* 30 November 2012

4   Stuart Waiton, *Snobs Law: Criminalising Football Fans in an Age of Intolerance,* (Take a Liberty Scotland, 2012), p.86.

Lafferty and Steven Davis, or Catholics Jörg Albertz and Nacho Novo, there is little fear in suggesting the latter two would win easily. This isn't a support which gets together to hurt Catholics, the Irish or Celtic fans, and if any sub-group ever did they would be challenged and ostracised. Of course, this doesn't mean individuals can't do something idiotic, but it's not culturally acceptable. Verbal stupidity rarely turns into action and the vast majority of Rangers fans hold the same moral views as the rest of Scotland.[5] The same is true for Celtic supporters.

Specifically targeting Catholics (or Protestants for that matter) with violence does happen in Scotland but, as the *Religiously Aggravated Offending in Scotland 2011–12* report points out, it is a very rare occurrence since most of the abuse is verbal. In addition, the victims are mostly police officers, workers or the 'community' (i.e. singing in the street) and so:

> This suggests that for the majority of charges it is unlikely the accused knew the religious affiliation/belief of the victim at the time of incident and that the religious abuse was more arbitrary in nature.[6]

In all of the cases combined, just four per cent of the 876 charges were assault. Fifty-eight per cent of the total figure was against Catholicism and 40 per cent against Protestantism. (Note the -isms since the police do not keep a record of the religion of the perpetrator or victim. It should also be noted that in the same period of 2011–12 there were 5,389 racist incidents.)[7]

It is because violence is rare, and sectarianism is mostly absent from politics, the criminal justice system, education, housing, welfare or the media, that there is such a focus on football songs. But here is the change: we used to hear about the 'Old Firm problem' but this is no longer the case. Celtic are rarely used as an example of bigotry, and the belief that both sides are just as bad as each other has been replaced by the overwhelming focus on Rangers. So did Celtic fans stop their anti-British or anti-Protestant songs and chants? Do they no longer delve into glorification of IRA terrorism? The answer to that is no, not completely. As with Rangers fans,

---

5 Having to point out the average Rangers fan has the same views on violence as the average Scot, is itself a sign that they are often badly stereotyped and dehumanised.

6 Amy Goulding and Ben Cavanagh, *Religiously Aggravated Offending in Scotland 2011–12*, Scottish Government Social Research 2012, www.scotland.gov. uk/Resource/0040/00408745.pdf, 23 November 2012

7 *Racist Incidents Recorded by the Police in Scotland, 2011-12*, Statistical Bulletin, Crime and Justice Series, www.scotland.gov.uk/Resource/0041/ 00411004.pdf, 11 December 2012

sectarianism is much rarer at home and less common among the away support, but vestiges still remain. Yet Celtic fans are largely ignored, sometimes defended and even praised, while condemnation for Rangers fans has increased.

The question is why? To answer that, we need to look at the description of the two 'groups' that are often assumed as opposing each other. On one side there are those who conflate Celtic, Irish Republicanism and Catholicism and on the other we have Rangers, British Unionism and Protestantism. By no means do the majority of people take on these concepts in full or to the same degree, and many not at all, but there is no doubt that a fusion of football, religion and nationality regularly happens. It's objectively a bit mad (or maybe completely mad) but just because it doesn't make sense to believe that a football team, religion and nationality are a single (or related) form of identity, is no basis for denying that many believe it to be true. None of this is sectarian, but when it is taken to extremes all of these identities become the source of sectarianism in Scotland, not just religion. As Dr Stuart Waiton of the University of Abertay says:

> It is often unclear what is being discussed when concerns about sectarianism are raised. Historically, it is understood as a religious problem; but there are the additional, and arguably more important, political elements associated with Irish Republicanism and British Unionism.[8]

Yet if it is assumed that sectarianism is only a problem of religious hatred then we are only seeing a smaller part of a larger issue. Religious sectarianism is the greatest taboo, while what is often called 'political sectarianism' is ignored. The written submission by the Association of Chief Police Officers in Scotland (ACPOS), to the Scottish Parliament's Justice Committee for the Offensive Behaviour at Football and Threatening Communications Bill, pointed out the focus on religious sectarianism is detrimental to defeating all sectarianism because:

> There would not appear to be scope to capture, other than to badge it under inciting public disorder, those who sing or chant **politically** [sic] sectarian messages that are pro/anti IRA, UVF, UDA, Fenian, Hun etc that are intended to offend other people.[9]

8 Stuart Waiton, *Snobs Law: Criminalising Football Fans in an Age of Intolerance*, (Take a Liberty Scotland, 2012), p.75.

9 *Written submission from the Association of Chief Police Officers in Scotland Football Sub Group* to the Scottish Parliament's Justice Committee, www.scottish.parliament.uk/S4_JusticeCommittee/Inquiries/OB60._ACPOS_Football_Sub_Group.pdf, 26 August 2011

Whether we should be condemning or arresting people for bad words in crowds is not the issue for this chapter. If Scottish society deems there should be a zero-tolerance approach to sectarianism then that should apply to everyone, without double standards. Yet many of the same people who would have a teenager jailed for chanting about the UVF defend IRA chants on the grounds that they are political. Violent or discriminatory anti-Irishness is sectarian and/or racist, while anti-Britishness is regarded by some as just an opinion or part of a 'struggle'? Calling someone a 'Fenian' is the worst form of bigotry, unless, it would seem, the offender is wearing a Celtic strip.

This is not a defence of any of the above. It is all moronic, but because there is a focus on Rangers fans, while others are seen as less of a problem, then not only is natural justice forgotten, but the anti-sectarian message is distorted. If you largely report on one 'side' and ignore the other, you create an environment in which one form of bigotry becomes *the* form of bigotry, while the rest goes unnoticed and a vicious cycle starts that cannot be stopped. Religious sectarianism is evil, while political sectarianism is bad, but 'not really bigotry'. The victim becomes lost in abstract definition. As if it matters to the child bullied or the man chased by thugs whether those who despise him do so because of their football team, religion or the political history of Ireland.

As offensive songs and symbols from Rangers fans come largely from the Unionist tradition of Northern Ireland, the more extreme expressions can touch on religious sectarianism, while some Celtic fans, through their association with violent Republicanism, will sometimes move into political sectarianism. Both can be appalling, but because of the boundaries society has deemed bigotry must be boxed into, it is Rangers who are in the spotlight even when the political sectarianism of Celtic fans (or call it any name you want since it doesn't matter) is just as bad or goes further. It ends up with the vilest form of hatred hiding behind nothing more than, 'it's not sectarianism'.

Let's try a little thought-experiment to explain further. Imagine if thousands of Rangers fans paid to enter legal music concerts at one of Glasgow's highest profile venues to listen to a 'Rangers and British' music band. There they are led by the group to chant pro-UVF slogans and openly sing about 'snipers', 'mortars', 'petrol bombs' and proudly boast that they should kill the Irish. Politicians and the police would be falling over themselves to condemn it. Arrests would be made and it would be front-page news for weeks. There would be no doubt it is sectarian, and even racist, to suggest people should leave the country or be murdered.

Yet this very thing happens in Scotland today with the knowledge of many within the police, political class and anti-sectarian charities. The only difference is that some of the bands and concert-goers wear Celtic strips and declare their love for Ireland.

One particularly obnoxious ditty, among many, is 'The SAM song'. This is no tribute to a man called Sam, instead it is an acronym for 'Surface to Air Missiles'. In the 21st century, Scottish police and Glasgow City Council allow concert-goers in their thousands to glorify 'the Ra', sing about missiles downing British Army helicopters and 'armalites' murdering 'coppers' in between songs about Celtic and the 'Huns'. Worst of all is the incredible line in the song that 'the Brits will never leave us until they're blown away'. In a 2012 letter from Strathclyde Police to Humza Yousaf MSP, currently the Scottish Government's Minister for External Affairs and International Development, the police advised that the Procurator Fiscal would not take any action against such bigotry because:

> the [SAM] song was being sung within a venue, to an audience who had paid specifically to attend and therefore would not be offended. [...] Clearly had this type of music been played in public, on a street, or in a football stadium, or in circumstances where there would be a strong likelihood of provoking or instigating a disturbance or disorder, then the matter would be treated differently.[10]

One wonders why paying into a public music concert is any different to paying into a public football match, or why being offended should play a defining part in the police or procurator fiscal's view of the law. A music concert where the song lyrics included 'the Irish will never leave us until they're blown away' would never merit such a despicably weak response.

'The SAM song' is a particularly clear-cut form of double-standards, but there are more. When footballer Scott McLaughlin of Ayr United was reported to have posted a message on the internet which read 'kill all Huns' there was little moral outrage. Incredibly, a few weeks before that *The Scottish Sun* pointed out that Aberdeen FC players Michael Paton and Zander Diamond 'apologised for posting anti-Protestant comments on Facebook when the Pope visited Scotland'.[11] Again, no arrests and no

---

[10] Letter from Deputy Chief Constable of Strathclyde Police Campbell Corrigan, to Humza Yousaf, Member of the Scottish Parliament, 19 March 2012.

[11] Alan Carson, 'Soccer star in kill all huns rant', *The Scottish Sun*, 22 October 2010

censure from politicians or the football authorities. It's highly unlikely that any of the above three said anything that was *really* meant, or should be acted upon, but they still get treated differently from a Rangers player or fan who is equally stupid. When former Rangers reserve goal-keeper Grant Adam made a sectarian remark he was arrested, charged and found guilty.[12] The arrest was even a lead story on TV news. More than one first-team Scottish footballer is verbally sectarian and nothing happens yet a single Rangers reserve player gets the full weight of the law and media.

While Rangers fans are shown zero tolerance, the behaviour of Celtic fans is often ignored or defended, even when the offence is the same or worse. With modern technology it is all too easy to view videos or pho-tographs that clearly show the hypocrisy. There have been photographs of banners at Celtic Park with lines taken from songs about the IRA, yet it is tolerated. Videos showing Celtic supporters shouting 'up the Ra' at away games in Europe or screaming 'go home ya Huns', 'murdering bas-tards' and 'Brits out now' to British Army troops at Arsenal's Emirates Stadium, are there for any journalist or anti-hate organisation to view. There are even ones showing hundreds, maybe thousands, of Celtic fans greeting Rangers players as they enter Celtic Park shouting the most des-picable abuse. Not only are they three feet in front of the stewards, but the same distance away from numerous police officers who stand by and watch, listen and do nothing to those screaming at the top of their voice against the 'Hun bastards', 'Orange C**ts', 'Dirty Orange Bastards', 'Paedophiles' and 'Rapists'. If the police and stewards watch this sectarianism against Rangers players and do nothing, what else is being ignored?

Away from footballers and the fans there is still, in my opinion, a level of hypocrisy and double standards within academia, politics and journalism that can shock. *The Sunday Herald* newspaper published an article in 2009 claiming that:

> A study into sectarianism funded with public money has been questioned after it emerged that one of its authors [Fatima Uygun] is a member of a pro-IRA Celtic FC fan group.[13]

When the Scottish Government were questioned as to whether they still

[12] 'Rangers goalkeeper Grant Adam fined £500 for sectarian song', *Daily Record*, 5 May 2012

[13] Paul Hutcheon, 'Author of sectarian study is member of pro-IRA fanzine', *Sunday Herald*, 13 December 2009

supported the findings of the report they replied that the research should be judged 'regardless of the individual views of those involved in delivering it.'[14]

Celtic director and ex-Labour MP Brian Wilson wrote in *The Scotsman* that he sang a song about IRA member Kevin Barry at Hillsborough Castle, the Queen's residence in Northern Ireland.[15] Wilson is no bigot, but what would happen if a Rangers supporting MP had sang 'Derry's Walls' because he was at the Irish Head of State's residence in Dublin? Wilson also signed off the article with 'let the people sing'. This, coincidentally, is the well-known title of an 'Irish rebel' song often sung by a band called The Wolfe Tones. The same group who have albums like 'Rifles of the IRA' and who once created a music video inside Celtic Park for a song which had a catchy chorus of 'up the Ra'.

Former First Minister Jack McConnell, who prided himself on his zero-tolerance of sectarianism, especially at Ibrox, was the subject of a *Sunday Times* article which claimed the 'first minister assisted sectarian groups in the face of police advice' by writing to Strathclyde police officers to help Republican bands. The article goes on to say that:

> The marchers planned to pass a Rangers' supporters pub and the local Orange hall and police had been warned that it would be petrol-bombed. It is understood McConnell's letter makes it clear he wanted the police to justify their decision in order to help the bands reapply for another march. [And] the republican bands' websites glorify IRA terrorism and are littered with anti-Protestant abuse.[16]

Irish journalist Phil Mac Giolla Bhain might not be well-known outside the web, but he is someone who Celtic fans idolise in worrying numbers. He is relentless in constantly stating that Rangers fans are a 'klan'[17] and the source of much, if not all, anti-Catholic bigotry in Scotland. Yet, without irony, he can write:

> Consider this scenario. A commercial provider of childcare, say, with

---

[14] Letter from Iain Richardson, Equalities & Sport Directorate, Scottish Government to John DC Gow, 15 November 2010

[15] Brian Wilson, 'Let the people sing – yes, even football supporters', *The Scotsman*, 30 November 2011

[16] Lucy Adams, 'Minister agreed to help IRA supporters', *Sunday Times*; 20 October 2002

[17] Phil Mac Giolla Bhain, 'Charlie and the klan', www.philmacgiollabhain.ie/charlie-and-the-klan/, 5 March 2013

twenty nurseries employed known paedophiles and then moved those child abusers to other crèches and day-care centres within the company if a parent complained and the abuser was free – within the organisation – to abuse again. [sic] Had that happened then the CEO of that day-care provider would be in prison. The Catholic Church, in Ireland and across the planet, ran a gulag of child abuse facilities. The CEO wears a funny hat he is called the 'Pope' and he was once in the Hitlerjugend.[18]

Once again, offensiveness is defined by who says it, rather than what is said. One wonders what Phil Mac Giolla Bhain would do if any Rangers fan had written that the Catholic Church ran a 'gulag of child abuse facilities' or mocked the Pope's attire?

To be fair on journalism, although he is very popular among Celtic fans, Phil Mac Giolla Bhain isn't 'mainstream'. If there is one journalist who is well known for his strong views on Rangers and sectarianism, it is Graham Spiers. He not only set the ball rolling on the idea that Rangers fans are worse (although no criteria has ever been given) but he went much further and started using stereotypes himself. Some Rangers supporters are demonised as 'unarguably the most socially-backward fans in British football'[19]; they are a 'white underclass,'[20] 'cavemen'[21] or a 'sub-species'.[22]

He seems unaware that if you use intemperate and dehumanising language then readers who want an excuse to believe Rangers fans are not like them will gladly take it. And believing others are not like you is, ironically, the very essence of bigotry. So why does someone who genuinely despises stereotypes and group demonisation do that very thing? The answer is in mistaking group mythology for reality and forgetting that the individual must be judged on what they say and do, not on what their ancestors did or to what group they belong.

For many, the Celtic identity which becomes fused with Catholicism and Ireland is seen as noble. Celtic fans are perceived as the victims

---

[18] Phil Mac Giolla Bhain, 'An Irish Gulag', www.philmacgiollabhain.ie/an-irish-gulag/, 20 May 2009

[19] twitter.com/GrahamSpiers/status/49851675992797184

[20] Graham Spiers, 'Rangers Supporters are fast running out of excuses', *The Times*, 9 November 2009

[21] Graham Spiers, 'Embarrassed on and off pitch, Players were found wanting, but so were the fans', *The Herald*, 6 November 2003

[22] Graham Spiers, 'Force to be reckoned with', *Scotland on Sunday*, 29 August 1999

regardless of their individual wealth or power, while the Rangers identity, fused with 'triumphalist' Protestantism and 'Imperial' Britain, is to be despised and mocked. Needless to say none of this is real to people doing their shopping, having a joke with their work colleague or falling in love. No-one is oppressed because of their nationality, religion or sports team in Scotland. You can't tell if someone supports Rangers or Celtic by looking at the car they drive or how much money they have in their wallet. There are no barriers in real life, only in the romantic anecdotes some people tell each other, yet many fall for it.

Yet, Graham Spiers is far from wrong on everything. He often points out that there are bigoted songs among some Rangers fans and that many of those people subscribe to a faux Protestantism and Unionism. Saying that, whether you like it or not, is perfectly proper and correct. The problem is that Spiers, and many like him since it's hardly a one-man band, only look one way. They query religion and politics in football at Ibrox, but laud it as a positive for Celtic. It often becomes less about anti-sectarianism and more about imposing a way of thinking, and leads some within the Rangers support becoming even more defensive about their identity.

For example, if you were to read the remarks of a Rangers fan who believes he is no longer allowed to express his non-sectarian and legal British and Protestant identity at football:

> One of the first remarks I ever heard being uttered with passion about Rangers was predictably in self-defence. I've heard it many times since and will go on hearing it until the end. It consists of three words which almost constitute a criminal defence of a club who are forever on the back foot because of their racial and religious heritage.
>
> [...] Rangers were a club founded by Protestants, who were driven by a Protestant sense of mission that was nothing if not admirable, yet the very mention of this evolved into something that was almost to be detested. Even in our sensitive times, some of us still felt wary of this because a loss of a sense of history seemed tantamount to a loss of collective identity.
>
> [...] The umbilical link between Rangers and British Protestantism, perversely, does not deserve to be disparaged, let alone erased. Instead, it deserves to be celebrated and cherished.[23]

If you are a Rangers fan do those words make you proud or embarrassed?

---

[23] Graham Spiers, 'Catholic guilt a heavy cross for the Celtic sons of Ireland', *Scotland on Sunday*, 10 September 2000

Does it explain your 'people', with their religion and nationality or is it a sign of a naked cave-man tribalism clothed in fine silks? If you are a non-Rangers fan, are such platitudes fine or do they confirm your belief that the Gers are not interested in football and are only concerned with an exclusive racial and religious belief-system?

When you realise these three paragraphs are not the rambling of some Neanderthal Rangers fan who wishes to bring religion, nationalism and 'racial heritage' into a sport, but the published work of Graham Spiers – and the only difference is that Celtic, Catholic and Ireland have been replaced by Rangers, Protestant and Britain – then everything changes. It might have been a misdirection, but in one broad stroke the viewpoint of many readers, and your opinion of Graham Spiers, might be shifted in a way endless argument would not. Especially when you discover he has written articles on the 'traditions of Rangers' where he questions the Gers fans for bringing religion and nationality into football:

> It is hard in the modern world to come out and say, "Rangers should be British and Protestant!" without sounding a bit like a caveman. But this is what they [the Rangers fans] are getting at.[24]

Notice that even if bringing Britain and Protestantism into football is great or ridiculous, it is not bigotry. The sneering at the 'underclass' shines through as we move from anti-sectarianism into nothing more than personal opinion. This movement goes unnoticed because for Graham Spiers it is always personal opinion. Yet while Rangers fan culture must be wrong, the deference for the mythology that surrounds Celtic, as well as the belief that sectarianism is largely a religious phenomenon, has led Spiers to make excuses. He has penned no less than three articles defending pro-Irish Republican Celtic fans like the Green Brigade, and sometimes questioning the motives of others for complaining about their IRA chants.[25] Although he makes it clear he detests IRA songs (and without irony we should believe him), he still says the issue can be complex due to some believing Celtic are, 'a symbol of the historic struggle of the Irish.' And that:

> Having stated that I detest IRA chants, I also know that such slogans are a complication, in Glasgow as elsewhere.[26]

---

[24] Graham Spiers, 'Vocal minority do not speak for the modern Rangers supporter', *The Times*, 19 January 2009

[25] Graham Spiers, 'The Green Brigade is wrongly portrayed', *The Times*, 21 November 2011

[26] Graham Spiers, 'Spiers on Sport: what to do with the Green Brigade?', *The Herald*, 19 February 2013

Does it ever occur to him that the 'struggle' of the Irish being acted out in 21st century Scottish sport is as 'faux' as the religious nonsense or that it is the same 'struggle' that Rangers fans are also referring? But worse, he also says this while admitting the pro-IRA chanting by Celtic fans is a reference to terrorists, and not a 100 year old war of independence:

> It doesn't sound very convincing these days to argue that, when Celtic fans chant about the IRA, they are in fact referring to an Irish liberation movement of nearly 100 years ago, rather than the terror group of recent times. This is a semantic we can do without.[27]

Ironically, far from doing without semantics, dividing behaviour that has the same source, intent and result becomes nothing but semantics. Even if sectarianism was a purely religious phenomenon and only Rangers fans sang sectarian songs, it is no less heinous to glorify terrorist killers because someone says it is 'political' or 'not sectarian'. There can't be anything less part of the political system or more sectarian than killing innocent people because they were British and/or Protestant.

But because our society has become ready to accept slogans rather than nuanced reality, singing a song promoting religious discord is seen as evil because it *may* lead to violence, while singing a song promoting terrorist groups like the IRA who *have* committed violence, is complicated. The only difference is how those symbols and songs are labelled – not the intent. Unfortunately, this type of irrational thinking is widely shared by quite a few journalists and politicians, including many Celtic fans.

As Graham Walker, Professor of Political History at Queen's University Belfast, says:

> There is among many Celtic cheerleaders, a categorical refusal to face up to the reality of the IRA campaign as a grubby sectarian war of attrition that got nowhere. [...] People who sing about Thompson guns, broad black brimmers, and raids on police barracks, [...] have no right to lecture others about the songs they sing. These are the songs sung at Celtic Park, not 'She moved through the Fair', 'Danny Boy', 'Galway Bay' or 'The Mountains of Mourne'. [...] It is, in short, about anti-Britishness rather than pro-Irishness.[28]

Of course there are many more examples when it comes to looking at the whole issue of sectarianism and hypocrisy for which books, never

---

[27] Graham Spiers, 'I don't see how you can muzzle club's cultural roots', *The Times*; 26 September 2011

[28] Graham Walker, *It's Rangers for me?*, (Fort Publishing Ltd, 2007), p.87.

mind chapters, could be written. Many pretend they are finally sorting out Rangers' bigotry when they are only following their own tribalism. Others are self-proclaimed neutrals who seem unwilling to test their basic assumptions and who unwittingly give shelter to the very hatred they despise. Yet the point here is not a plea for victimhood, but a request for parity within the law, the media and the political class. It is certainly not an appeal for the same blindness towards Rangers that happens else-where – quite the opposite.

Let's not forget Rangers didn't knowingly sign Catholics from around the 1920s to the 1980s, and while few fans today are real bigots, some of the symbolism and songs haven't moved forward. Pretending that Rangers have no issues is not only counter-factual but harmful. Inventing a false narrative so that it can be defended not only denies Rangers' history in full, but leaves the club open to attack from those who wish it harm and ensures that it cannot grow in the 21st century. Professor Graham Walker has passionately and eloquently pointed this out before. In *It's Rangers for Me?* he warns of the club:

> finding it problematic to construct a positive vision of the future that would build on life-affirming aspects of history [rather than] into a cul-tural and political cul-de-sac.[...] Dilemmas, controversies and prob-lems of course remain. Many Rangers fans now complain that any song or chant in praise of the traditional image of the club is considered fair game for the forces of political correctness and those who make a career out of a supposed campaign against sectarianism. Their defen-siveness can be understood and maybe sympathised with in certain cases – it is often a reaction to an agenda set by the Celtic-minded – but it remains dangerous to the health of the club. The issues need to be faced up to openly and radically. It is important to feel that you can be passionate about your club and its history [but] it behoves us all to resist the descent into intolerance and the attractions of a defiance which can only be futile. There is too much at stake for our club.[29]

As the late Garry Lynch said:

> I don't support Rangers because they are, or rather were, a Protestant institution. I want eleven winners rather than eleven Protestant losers. We don't know what half the team are and we don't care, and just about everybody who goes to Ibrox now feels the same.[30]

---

[29] Graham Walker, *It's Rangers for me?*, (Fort Publishing Ltd, 2007), p.58–59.
[30] Ronnie Esplin, *Down the Copland Road*, (Argyll Publishing, 2000), p.38.

This is someone who rarely missed a game from the youths up[31] – a real Rangers man – yet he couldn't care less about the religion of the players. The vast majority of the support completely agree, yet while no-one would think of stereotyping individual Britons (including Scots), Irish, Roman Catholics and Protestants – the very identities that some Rangers and Celtic fans cherish – for their incredibly bloody history of murder; torture; physical, mental and sexual child abuse; racism; sectarianism and general hatred, many will stereotype a sports club and supporters for briefly being caught up in the very problems those religions and national identities created.

It is the extremists within these cultures who have damaged Scotland with their dogma – not a football team. But with an ignorance of history and a media which had fallen for the line that political sectarianism was somehow more noble or less problematic than religious sectarianism, real life was thrown under the bus and one set of idiots were demonised while the others were ignored or protected. Add to the mix a weak Rangers who continued to grow smaller with each condemnation, the financial calamity created a perfect storm culminating in a 2012 in which most of Scotland believed that Rangers FC was sectarianism defined. If most Scots were repeatedly told that this sports team uniquely represented bigotry as a culture (although we have seen that is not the case) then it is no wonder they wanted the club destroyed. The financial problems were just the excuse to moralise and act.

But for all the hypocrisy and ignorance surrounding Rangers and bigotry, the club itself failed to act properly to protect itself and the majority of fans. Not only should they have put a massive amount of energy into ensuring the minority who occasionally shame the club were stopped once and for all, but they refused to engage in protecting the brand and through their inaction allowed others to turn the club into a pariah. If you let those who wish to do you harm define your image to wider society, then it is little surprise that the picture painted is the worst it could be.

Yet it's not all doom and gloom. There is a growing awareness that blaming football fans for bigotry, or focusing on religious sectarianism is too narrow. In an article in *The Herald*, the Scottish Government's new 'anti-bigotry czar', Dr Duncan Morrow from the University of Ulster,

---

[31] Douglas Dickie, 'Worldwide tributes to biggest Glasgow Rangers fan', *Rutherglen Reformer*, 18 February 2009

pointed out that 'it's not just about religion'. Reporter Gerry Braiden correctly adds that:

> [such] views will clash with many in Scotland who believe that unless there is an explicit reference to another's faith, insults, derogatory terms and even songs in support of paramilitary organisations are not sectarian. [For example] court cases involving either Ulster Loyalist or Irish Republican songs have seen the sectarian element disregarded because of an absence of reference to faiths.[32]

This is a start, but for Rangers everything must change. Instead of cowering under the topic of sectarianism, they should take it on completely and lead from the front both verbally and financially. Not signing Catholics over a 60 year period was wrong, but what happened in the past is the past. There is no need to deny that this is a part of the Rangers story or run from it in self-flagellation. The history of Rangers is ours, in total, both good and bad, victory or loss. Pretending everything was either perfect or terrible is infantile. Embracing it would allow the club to open up the debate and demand that others live up to the same standards that they want from Rangers. It's only because the club fears being called bigoted that it can be bullied and have its position distorted. The first half of 2012 might have been a freak few months, but it showed that being painted as a source and keeper of sectarianism only allows others to take advantage. Rangers need to commit to a pincer movement against the minority of bigots within the support, and also those in wider society who blame the club for sectarianism while ignoring or defending bigotry themselves. If they don't they will always be on the back-foot to those who, through ignorance or tribalism, still hate them.

---

[32] Gerry Braiden, 'Anti-bigotry czar warns sectarianism is classless', *The Herald*, 7 January 2013

CHAPTER XI

Foundations for the Future

ROSS EJ HENDRY

LONG BEFORE CRAIG Whyte arrived on the scene, ready to wreak his own brand of havoc on Rangers, there was a feeling held by sections of the Rangers support that the club was underachieving both on and off the pitch. The football and commercial operation looked tired after more than a decade of outsourcing and downsizing. Long gone were the days of cutting edge, some might say radical, marketing initiatives designed to swell the cash reserves of the club. Equally, the teams had become mundane. Yes, there were great moments and title wins. But the entertainment value on a week in, week out basis was debatable. From the stands it looked as though Rangers had failed to move with the times on and off the pitch. In fairness, both budgets and commercial viability were restricted. First, as a result of Sir David Murray's long, drawn-out exit from the club and second, by the aggressive repayment options Lloyds Banking Group presented the club with in settling its borrowings. In addition, a ponderous HMRC inquiry and tribunal investigating the use of Employee Benefit Trusts was unhelpful. On top of this, our bitter rivals were in the same division. This placed extra onus on the need to win immediately: it was all so obviously short term.

Through their determination to see Rangers punished, the club's adversaries were not only attacking its future, they were attacking our past. And, when they attacked our history it was only natural that we defended it vigorously. This was our club, our history, our traditions. It was stories passed by a grandfather to a grandson as they poured over newspaper cuttings spanning decades; each turn of a page accompanied by whispers of Meiklejohn and Caldow. The now grown man, sitting with his father as he reminisced, lubricating the memory with a bottomless glass of Speyside, about the night a Bayern Munich side – boasting seven players who, two years earlier, won the World Cup for Germany – came to Ibrox in 1972 and left with their tails between their legs. And how that was the last time that he and Jimmy stood on the terrace together. It was about an embrace shared between brothers an Atlantic Ocean away from Florence and the subsequent transatlantic journey to

Manchester that was planned without thought to finance or responsibilities. Not a chance it was going to be taken from us. In fact, it became a ludicrous suggestion to think they could take memories away. Somehow erase time. The more they tried, the more we resisted. The more they tried to divide us, the more galvanized we became.

Finally, on 27 July 2012, the club's registration and membership transfer to the new holding company secured our history and our future. In the weeks that followed, primarily as a result of the incredible loyalty of the support, it became obvious that our immediate financial future was also secure with the Ibrox faithful purchasing an incredible 38,000 season books. With that we could gladly wave goodbye to the barren no man's land that we had existed in for months. A sense of relief and reflection immediately washed over the entire support. There was a sense of jubilation that one particular battle in the war had been won and we would stand, over 49,000 strong, to welcome league play back to Ibrox. But in football, time for extended reflection is often hard to come by.

Within a matter of weeks, and once we had come to terms with the fact that we had been demoted to the lowest tier of professional football, the question wasn't 'what are we going to do' but 'what can we do?' This truly is one of the most endearing things about the Rangers support. They are at odds with playing the victim card. It is just not in our makeup. If we are kicked we take it and come up from the mat swinging, more resolute and more determined than before. One is reminded of Theodore Roosevelt's famous excerpt from Citizenship in a Republic, delivered at the Sorbonne in 1910, when thinking of the club and the support:

> It is not the critic who counts; not the man who points out how the strong man stumbles, or where the doer of deeds could have done them better. The credit belongs to the man who is actually in the arena, whose face is marred by dust and sweat and blood; who strives valiantly; who errs, who comes short again and again, because there is no effort without error and shortcoming; but who does actually strive to do the deeds; who knows great enthusiasms, the great devotions; who spends himself in a worthy cause; who at the best knows in the end the triumph of high achievement, and who at the worst, if he fails, at least fails while daring greatly, so that his place shall never be with those cold and timid souls who neither know victory nor defeat.

We could all sense it. There was an opportunity presenting itself, an opportunity not only to rise up from the very bottom of Scottish football but to come back stronger, leaner and more professional on all fronts. Worry about the future subsided to make way for excitement and a new found optimism.

In order to hypothesise about the future of Rangers you have to take into account the engrained norms and mores of the club. Opinions on this vexed subject could, and have, filled volumes of text. And, not just from the football perspective but how this wonderful institution has shaped, and continues to shape, the socio-political landscape of Scotland. What constitutes the fabric of Rangers FC is always a matter of closely guarded opinion. These opinions are cultivated from the first time you see the famous royal blue strip with the letters RFC intricately intertwined on the left breast, through the first time you come to the top of the stairs, from the gantry below, to see the magnificent sight of a full Ibrox. They are debated and contested across Scotland and the world every moment of every day. To steal a phrase, the sun never sets on the Rangers support.

Obviously the footballing culture at Rangers has evolved over time. From the Rangers 'tourists' of 1905, so revered by Hugo Meisl, the famous coach of Mattias Sindelar and the Austrian *Wunderteam,* to the pragmatic approach of Walter Smith over a century later. That being said, there are certain things that can be distilled from over 140 years of history that define a Rangers style. We are a club that values creative, direct wing play and skilful central midfielders who can 'mix it' as well as dribble and pass efficiently. The base of any successful Rangers side always has a strong, dominating centre back as cerebral as he is tough in the tackle. Centre forwards that are as powerful as they are prolific have dominated Scottish football wearing royal blue. It is with simple ideals that the future of the club should be defined and it is with precision that they must be executed.

It is hardly ground-breaking to suggest that Rangers' youth teams should be playing in the same style as the first team. The question for those running the football operation at the club is if not now, when? For the first time since the establishment of professional football in the UK, the pressure on Rangers to win every game has been lifted. Yes, the support still expects to win every match and to do so with *some* authority. However, the standard of the opposition as we travel through the lower reaches of Scottish football could hardly be described as daunting, with all due respect to the endeavour, dedication and passion of the Peterhead's and Queens Park's of the world. This should allow us to be exploratory in our approach to refining the Rangers footballing philosophy. It should also allow us to bed in a group of youth players that become at one with it in a senior team environment.

The journey through the depths of Scottish football should see the nurturing of our youth in the football ideal while looking to the first team for examples of how dedication to the philosophy and hard work will reap benefits. It is hardly a leap to suggest that players currently in the youth system look at the likes of Lewis Macleod and think, 'that can be me'. Furthermore, there is a palatable inclination from the support to be patient on this adventure. As long as there looks to be forward momentum they will identify with the 'growing up' process on the pitch. Indeed, seeing some of 'our own' lead us to our 55th top division title is the wish of every Rangers supporter. It is, however, the club's duty to instil a hunger and a work ethic in these young men. The confines of Auchenhowie, a facility of indisputable class, are the perfect place to hone talent. It is the club's duty to prepare them appropriately and create a system that allows them smooth passage from youth to senior football. A young player's first touch, movement off the ball and technical quality should be automatic. They should find safe harbour in the system and it should have familiarity at all levels of the club.

Ultimately, we want to see forward progress driven by clear thinking. Make no mistake about it, apart from success on the pitch, the crucial benefit of having a youth structure that produces successful teams and talented footballers is commercial return. Not only does the average supporter identify with the lad that comes through the youth ranks, but good players, in successful teams, demand higher transfer fees. Of course, having a replacement is vital to continued success. It is always a risk transferring a youth player from the reserve team to the first team. However, that risk is considerably reduced if the newly promoted player has been playing in a similar system through his football adolescence. In the system, the player will gain a level of comfort that limits the normal levels of anxiety associated with graduating from youth to senior football.

At the moment Rangers do not have the technical staff capable of defining, implementing, refining and executing a root and branch rework of the football operation. Without considerable study and experience it is impossible to give a complete answer to what the set up should look like. However, there are numerous examples that afford us the luxury of suggesting alternatives. There is *Alcochete* (The Oven), the Sporting Club de Portugal academy in Portugal. When one of Europe's best-equipped football factories was being revealed in 2002, our old European sparring partners stated that this 250,000m^2 facility would form a 'strategic pillar' of the club. The scary thing is that this is a club that had produced Futre, Quaresma, Figo, Simão, Cristiano Ronaldo and a host of other players before the unveiling of this breathtaking facility. Alcochete produces forward players like the Ferrari compound at Maranello produces sports cars. The methodology is clear from Sporting – produce world class talent then reinvest in the facility. We also have examples of this sustainable model at the vaunted academies at Barcelona, Manchester United and Ajax, among a host of others. It is interesting to look at what happened to the Ajax model following the European Cup win of the mid-1990s. Instead of continuing with the time honoured tradition of investing in youth they went the opposite way toward talent acquisition. This coincided with a downturn in the club's fortunes both on and off the pitch. It is only now that they have returned to their traditional ways that we are starting to see the Ajax of old emerge. Yes, they have pending financial problems but they have assets in the form of players to help them deal with these issues.

It seems clear these systems have two indisputable things in common. First, they produce world class players. Second, and more important, there is a clear commitment from the clubs to invest in the conveyor belt of talent. It is absolutely integral to the way these clubs operate. It is quite clear that Rangers have yet to take this step. Again, this begs the question if not now, when we have a clean slate on both the financial and sporting fronts at the club, then when?

It is also common knowledge that there is a growing number of European clubs that have started to expand their player identification process beyond traditional scouting networks. For example, in the state of Texas alone, Liverpool, Manchester United and Chelsea (to name just three teams) have close links with youth club teams. This not only involves kids wearing the colours of the club in question, it involves direct input from the clubs into how the teams are coached and the standards that are sought after. In many cases it involves coaching staff from the youth teams visiting the home club's facilities in the UK to gain insight and knowledge into the most modern coaching techniques and ideas. With Rangers recently signing players from the USA, does it not beg the question as to why the club is not doing the same thing?

The simple fact is that Rangers have neglected an area of the football operation that is seen as key to many of the world's largest clubs. Instead of looking to the long term they have looked to short term fixes. This lack of foresight highlights a number of problems in the Rangers set up. There is no technical staff to execute a long term strategy. There is no player identification process in place to pinpoint the raw materials required. And, finally, there is no investment to support the design, implementation and management of a youth system befitting a modern day football club with any degree of aspiration. The old model is fraught with both financial problems and constraints. If Rangers do not look to fix it now then there are only two possible outcomes – overweighed investment in player acquisition which has already proven to be unsustainable or underweighted investment that will see the club become uncompetitive. Neither of these scenarios is particularly attractive and the reality for the club's owners is that the Rangers support, despite their loyalty over the last 12 months, will vote with their feet. The Board of Directors would be served well by having a long, hard look at how Rangers' system operates in comparison to the clubs they aspire to compete with in the long term. If they do not, then they face the very harsh reality that the returns they expect may not be easily realised.

If there are numerous improvements to be made to the footballing operation at Ibrox, then at least there are also ample opportunities. Essentially, the club is going from a situation where it was being broken up for parts, having them sold out the back door and the rusting chassis left on four cinder blocks, to an enviable situation of a clean financial slate. The new Board of Directors have *carte blanche* in identifying new profit streams and optimising existing ones in order to improve the commercial output. This is an incredibly advantageous position and a challenge that any business person would relish, particularly a business person that secured the assets of one of the world's great clubs for just £5.5m. However, as with the aforementioned football operation, you will only get out what you put in. In order for Rangers FC to reach their full potential off the pitch, those in control will have to invest in both human and financial resources. In any sort of commercial development or optimisation project looking for long term, meaningful output, it is absolutely essential that there is investment, up front, to realize the envisioned potential.

In the months that followed that historic day at Brechin, Charles Green and his Board of Directors started to make noises that were encouraging. We've often heard from Green, Ahmad and Stockbridge that Rangers FC is capable of incredible commercial performance. There were also signs that, as much as there was a degree of sabre rattling going on, they believed what they were saying. Shortly after the renewal of 38,000 season tickets, Rangers' chief executive started to float the idea of an IPO. This was successfully executed in December of 2012 when approximately £21m was raised from both supporters and institutional investors when the holding company was floated on the Alternative Investment Market (AIM). This sub-market allows smaller companies to float shares with a more flexible regulatory system. Companies regularly join AIM in order to gain growth capital and this is exactly what Rangers needed, not only to balance the books while the club climbed the divisions but also to start looking at some of the abovementioned opportunities. Of course, whether or not the current Board sees fit to invest some of that £21m in growing the brand remains to be seen. After a spike in the immediate aftermath of floatation, the stock is now performing in a stable manner which is admirable considering the UK is poised to enter its third recession in as many years. Charles Green and his Rangers partners put in the best performance seen at Ibrox in the past year in securing the level of investment they did at the time they did.

Three months prior to the IPO the club signed a deal with Sports Direct. This saw the termination of the much maligned agreement between JJB and Sir David Murray which was signed in 2006. With hindsight, the motivation for Murray to enter into a partnership with JJB was clear; up-front cash injection, yet again outsourcing an asset of the club. The Sports Direct deal appears to be an upgrade on the previous retail deal and they are one of the largest sports apparel retailers in Europe. The improved reach alone should see an increase in revenue generated by the retail channel of the club. The irony of Sports Direct acquiring 60 stores from a JJB finding itself in administration was not lost on the more commercially alert members of the Rangers support. Once again we were served up evidence of how disastrous the second half of the Murray regime was for the club; short term, low value thinking. What we can be assured of, as evidenced by his actions so far, is that Charles Green will seek maximum value for its assets. Further evidence of this became apparent in November as the rumoured renaming of Ibrox started to gather steam. Approximately two months later, it became apparent that Sports Direct was the leading candidate to have their name incorporated in to Ibrox Stadium. This decision has polarised the support and there have been vocal and visual displays of protest from the Ibrox faithful against stadium renaming. Debating the issue is beyond the scope of this piece but it must be recognized that those running the club are once again looking to maximise returns. In isolation, this can only be a good thing. That the deal struck is mooted to be for only a year shows not only a keen negotiating streak but it also suggests Green knows the true value of Rangers assets. Giving them away cheaply is not an option.

Next on the menu for the executive team must be to fix the club's media department and the content it delivers. With the appointment of James Traynor as the Director of Communications, Green has proven that he is willing to hire expensive talent. Furthermore, when they have the resources and focus, the current team can produce excellent, unique content as we observed with *The Rising* documentary on RangersTV. Sadly, it is a fact that projects were put on hold and departmental budgets were adjusted to produce this documentary, suggesting the media department is under resourced. Live games have also been broadcast through RangersTV this year which, after initial teething problems, look to have improved considerably. There are numerous other opportunities, however, that remain to be explored. For example, there has been no movement on the back catalogue of games available to a RangersTV subscriber. This should be an easy fix. These should be made available for permanent purchase or for rental and the iTunes model is an easy one to replicate. To that point, the fact that RangersTV has not entered into an agreement with the Apple Store, the largest seller of digital content on the Internet, is baffling. Yes, Apple will ask for a slightly larger percentage of the margin available and yes it takes people away from the official club channel but, at the moment, there is no alternative. RangersTV does not offer, to my knowledge, downloadable content. And, even if it did, why would you not want to partner with a delivery method that allows global access and provides the content delivery vehicle for you? Punters could still access the official site but this gives a gargantuan, additional point of purchase.

Content delivery is another easy fix for the commercial team at Ibrox. A project should be started that looks to integrate the three existing online platforms that Rangers currently operate; the official site, RangersTV and The Rangers Megastore. A single sign-on process and true customer profile could instantly lead to increased time on site and purchase per visit rates. It would also allow increased insight into consumer behaviour, opinion and feedback. The amount of low hanging fruit available to the commercial team is reason to believe that the club's net revenue position looks a good bet to increase substantially in the coming years. Indeed, the very fact that someone from overseas cannot purchase match tickets on the site with any degree of regularity is a woeful miss from the club and is easily fixable. Why do Rangers supporters abroad have to watch live games via a desktop or laptop computer? Is it not apparent that content today simply must be functional across all platforms including mobile? Inside of three years since its launch, Apple sold over 100m iPad units. Yet, I cannot watch my club play live on my iPad! Again, easy fixes.

In the interest of balance, it must be said that the flow of communication from the club via social media channels has been exceptional under the stewardship of Robert Boyle. However, there is always room for improvement and the focus must be on increasing engagement and interaction with the club via social media. Robert Boyle, Andrew Dickson

FOUNDATIONS FOR THE FUTURE

and Lindsay Herron have all done impressive work within the Rangers media department. Given their performance over the past few years, under considerable duress and restriction, they should be afforded the opportunity to expand the scope of their operations. Writing regular blogs, hosting interactive Q and A sessions and even a nightly call-in show are all things the current media team should be given a chance to tackle. Not only would these actions allow the support to interact directly with the club, it would also allow for tighter control of the media output. This is not to suggest the message should be sycophantic. Quite the opposite, it should be open forum, thus making it engaging and desirable to tune-in to. In turn this reduces the support's reliance on the more traditional forms of media. If that is not enough, the advertising revenues should be all the reason required to explore this possibility. Succinctly, my frustration does not lie with the current level of output or those responsible for it. Rather they are focused on the current Board and whether or not they will invest in opportunities up front in order for the club to maximise all possible income potentials.

Nowhere is the need for investment more necessary than in optimising current brand/market combinations and developing new ones. For many years there has been talk about opportunities abroad and taking the Rangers brand international. Indeed, Charles Green has made many a mention of this on his whistle-stop tour around the world. In my opinion there is an opportunity to grow the brand internationally. However, before we develop the brand beyond the shores of the UK it is my contention that there is a job to be done at home. The Rangers brand has been damaged and those in charge of the strategic marketing and brand development at Ibrox should be looking closely at how to nurse it back to health. The distinct advantage they have is that the brand will still be valuable to an enormous amount of people: the Rangers support. What the club has to start doing is defining the brand again. What is the Ibrox tradition that Bill Struth spoke of in his famous speech? By defining that tradition you have begun to define the shared motivation of each and every Rangers supporter. Not only that, you have defined a potential supporter; someone that might not realize it yet but at heart is a Rangers supporter. The only way to truly define the Rangers brand is to research it appropriately and this research lies at the heart of every brand development exercise. In order to understand what attachment 50,000 people have to Rangers every other Saturday you need to talk to them. Again, this type of research requires substantial investment. The upside, however, is truly interesting. My argument is that currently we operate at a baseline level.

The club does not offer terrible services and products but it does not offer great services either.

At the moment, there is no improvement taking place at the central focal point: the match-day experience. Accessibility for those driving to the game should be looked at. A museum, a modernised shopping environment and both adult and family orientated facilities should be seriously considered. Connecting a museum with the history of Govan's industry or Scottish amateur athletics is a no brainer. Both are distinct pieces of the club's history and will help build a tangible foundation for the club moving forward. Associations with the local area and with purely sporting Scottish organisations can only serve the club well and will allow the outsider to understand that there is more to Rangers than just football.

In strictly commercial terms, there is no multi-channel approach to driving consumer purchase or brand message. In fact, there is no message to speak of at all and, as such, there is a definite limit to commercial revenue. Are Rangers a Scottish or a British club? Are Rangers a Unionist club? What is Rangers' relationship with Northern Ireland? What are the core values of Rangers FC? What principles was the club founded on? Yes, there will be varying opinions on each of these questions and that is no bad thing. However, to the outside observer there is no tangible, 'official' answer. In terms of brand development, the primary goal should be its definition. Once this has occurred, the previously mentioned museum experience would be incredibly helpful in looking to develop new brand/market combinations.

There are things that we know would come out of the aforementioned research. For example, the club is undeniably Scottish but is comfortable with Scotland's place in the Union. This Scottishness is something with intrinsic value in other markets because there are no other clubs from Scotland promoting it internationally. Yet, a short walk around Times Square in New York City and you will find a handful of Scottish pubs. Being Scottish is a desirable and interesting trait. The development team at Ibrox would be well served by focusing on the club's Scottishness when considering their approach to potential markets. The desire for authenticity and heritage are both on the rise as consumer trends and this should form the basis of the external communication of the strategy. Nowhere is this characteristic more marketable than in Canada and the United States where the Scottish disapora is most prominent. Furthermore, there are already organisations in place that can assist with entry into this market. One such body is the Scottish North American Business Council which has a remit of assisting Scottish businesses entering North

America. Rangers may look to enter this market through regionalised associations with prominent youth teams in areas such as Texas, California and New York, or even establishing specific Rangers youth academies.

In terms of fan base development and engagement, it is imperative that our deal with Puma contains key performance indicators around market penetration in the United States, Canada and other high potential markets. Puma simply must increase the sales volume of Rangers merchandise. There are various ways that this can be accomplished. First, they must increase distribution. Quite simply, Rangers strips and merchandise are not accessible or visible enough in foreign markets. This is now the responsibility of Puma as well as Rangers. If distribution and visibility go up then it is reasonably safe to assume that rate of sale and subsequently volume of sales will go up. Over and above growing distribution of merchandise and increasing the available points of purchase, there are ways to engage existing and prospective supporters. For example, if Rangers are releasing a new strip then it should be an occasion. A targeted third party executed event should take place, synchronised with the British reveal of the new strip, at Puma outlets in major urban centres across Canada and the United States. There is nothing to stop the top tier of these events featuring an official delegation from Rangers themselves. Manchester United recently started a campaign named 'I am United' aimed at bringing the club closer to its global fan base. This is exactly the type of engagement Rangers should be looking at, especially when we consider there are approximately 50 official Supporters Clubs already in North America.

Changed circumstances have brought with them remarkable opportunities. Both on and off the pitch, there is a clean slate and nothing but upside to realise. If Rangers need a tangible example of how a club can return from the brink of financial ruin to once again scale incredible heights it only need look at Borrussia Dortmund, its old sparring partner from previous European nights. In 2005, the German club stood on the precipice staring in to the abyss. Through hard work, organisation and adherence to the strategic vision the commercial and footballing operations found harmony and now coexist in the most productive fashion. Guillem Balague in his book *Pep Guardiola – Another Way of Winning* said, 'changing the answer is evolution, replacing the question is revolution'. It is quite clear to me that those who have designs on returning Rangers FC to former glories, and reaping the associated financial windfall, must rapidly start changing the question or the ultimate opportunity will pass us by.

CHAPTER XII

Rousing the Rangers Family

DAVID EDGAR

In waking a tiger, use a long stick.   MAO ZEDONG

LIFE IS PRIMARILY made up of normal days, but it's the abnormal ones
that history is interested in. And for those whose job it is to chronicle
the tale of our great club, 2012 was just absolutely packed with them.
Indeed, from the moment the news of Rangers' imminent move towards
administration broke, it seemed as though each passing day was trying to
outdo its predecessor. The utterly bizarre became the new reality as ever
more incredible events superseded each other with clinical regularity. Every
Bear who lived through that period will remember the ball of angst that
formed instantly in their stomach when they received a text message or
took a phone call. There was suddenly too much news to deal with; a
surfeit of rumour and innuendo, half-truths and all-too-real-truths. There
were lies mixed with facts. Suddenly people who could barely string a
coherent sentence together were financial experts, postulating on intricate,
arcane matters that they'd never let on about having a scholarly interest
in before. It melted your brain while you were trying to stop your heart
from breaking.

Another thing about history is that it is often said to have been written
by the winners. That's one area where the Rangers crisis was markedly
different. Firstly, there were no winners, certainly not among the story's
protagonists. Rangers ended up in the Third Division after the most traum-
atic year in our history. The Scottish Premier League clubs who put them
there now have to survive on significantly reduced finances. Traditional
media tore itself apart following, then most assuredly *not* following, new
media. Those same new media sites – best exemplified by the infamous
Rangers Tax Case blog – spoke proudly of being pioneering crusaders
fighting a conspiracy of silence, while at the same time viciously condemning and censoring anyone who dared to question their opinions. Pundits
gleefully stepped out from behind their thin veneer of impartiality to see
who could be the most eviscerating in their condemnation of Rangers FC
and everything to do with it, before desperately trying to cover their

modesty when the so-called 'Big Tax Case' verdict came in. The authorities seemed determined that nobody would ever take them seriously ever again. Appearing to lurch from one catastrophic piece of mismanagement to the next, they could not have made themselves look more hatefully foolish if they'd taken to delivering press conferences dressed as pirates. Bridges weren't so much burned as blown up. The SFA immediately made it clear it wanted to punish Rangers for what had happened to them, handing the club a £160,000 fine and a legally unenforceable transfer ban (which wasn't actually a sanction open to them.) The club, while on its knees, found that the authorities seemed determined to hinder any attempt to rise up off them. It is only speculation to assume this treatment wouldn't have been handed out to anyone else, but let's be honest; this wouldn't have happened to anyone else.

Of course, most history tends to be written *after* the events take place. This was another major contrast when it came to Rangers. At times, it appeared that just about every major decision had already been made, and that our football club was just about the only actor on stage who didn't know where the play was heading. The verdict was written before the trial commenced. Rangers were guilty of cheating. Rangers were to be punished and left, barely breathing if breathing at all, in the depths of Scottish football. Us follow followers were to be simultaneously ignored and jeered, a good trick but one most of our critics managed with aplomb. We were to be spoken about, certainly not to.

Yes, the landscape for professional football in this country at the end of 2012 was, unquestionably, much bleaker than when it started. But amongst all the wreckage, after all the pain, could we as a club have rediscovered something far more important? Because while it was not something we'd want to go through again – dear God, no – Rangers fans discovered something we'd misplaced during the tumultuous Sir David Murray era: our soul. I'd argue that the Rangers Family in 2012 became more than just a marketing term. For the first time in a long time, Rangers fans gathered together with more interest in our bonds than our differences.

To blame Murray for the change in fan culture at Ibrox during his reign is tempting, but it ignores the wider reality. Football as a whole changed during those two decades. The influx of money into the sport, the growth of television as the primary means of following a team and the changing nature of society saw to that. The fragmentation of the support was not unique to Rangers; indeed, at clubs all across the UK, older fans looked on with barely disguised distaste at the new breed of supporters. Those new supporters tended to be uninterested in the legacies of terracing that the previous generation were keen to preserve. Some of the elements we've lost from our game – violence, widespread drunkenness at matches, intolerance – no-one can reasonably miss. But we lost more abstract qualities along the way, particularly humour, perspective and the overarching sense of belonging that used to be an essential part of being a supporter.

The negative effects of this splintering were not immediately apparent, but over time many suspected that this lack of unity – and, more pertinently, having no recent history of collective activism – would prove damaging as the club began to come under sustained attack from its opponents.

Let me be clear here; I hate using terms like 'enemies' and 'attacks' when discussing what is, in essence, only a game. Football is supposed to be a leisure activity, a pastime. Football is supposed to be *fun*. But it most assuredly hasn't been fun in Scotland for a long time. And it is naïve to ignore the *realpolitik* of the situation. So many of us – and I've been as guilty of this as anyone else – invest so much emotionally in the game that it takes on entirely different levels of meaning. Is this right? No, not at all, but it happens and to deny that it does – or worse, to pretend when it suits your argument that it doesn't – is plain wrong.

The simple fact is that Rangers are important to many people on a scale few modern institutions can match. And those who targeted it were doing so with the obvious intent of causing as much pain to those people as they could. That strikes me as a funny sort of grown-up, but there is no doubt that we witnessed this phenomenon. Gers fans were left in no doubt what some of the politicians, journalists and opinion-formers of this country thought of them.

'Banter' is a hard thing to quantify, especially with a subject as emotive as football. But for the vast majority of Rangers fans, the overwhelming level of hatred that was poured over them during this period was genuinely shocking. Of course, as one of the biggest and best clubs in the country, a lot of it was to be expected, and was even reasonable – who doesn't like to see the big guy fall? It happens in every sport. And while many Rangers fans would not have appreciated it, being the butt of jokes was another expected and reasonable outcome. We'd have done the same. Anyone who says they wouldn't is fibbing. It's an inescapable part of football and it's never going to change.

What did come as a surprise to many was when it went beyond that. Fans of other teams didn't want Rangers simply humiliated; they wanted them dead. They wanted the club hounded out of business. They wanted the authorities to put the boot in as the club lay wounded, and with a compliant – indeed, complicit – media in tow, they set about screaming for what they called 'justice'. That they didn't actually know the crimes Rangers were accused of was merely incidental. We were guilty of *something*, we had to be, and we had to be brought down for it.

Probably the saddest part of the whole thing, from a personal perspective, was decent supporters of other clubs – and this includes Celtic – being so easily corralled by the more poisonous elements of their supports. That they couldn't even react with basic decency to the obvious suffering of people who were, in many cases, friends and colleagues simply because of the football team they followed reflects very poorly on them. The usual excuse – Rangers fans deserve this because Rangers fans are bigots – doesn't really stand up to much scrutiny. Simply put, if you knew one of these bigoted Rangers fans, why were you friends with them in the first place? But then, Rangers fans ceased to be individuals to these people, and their friends in the media, a long time ago, becoming instead an amorphous mass with collective ideas and beliefs assigned to them. I would say judging an entire group of people based on a single shared interest is much closer to bigotry than the perpetrators would ever have the insight to realise.

Rangers fans, we were told, had not shown enough contrition for what had happened. We were 'not sorry enough'. This was bizarre even by the looking-glass standards of Scottish football. It was akin to having a go at an assault victim for bleeding on the pavement. The fact that people were demanding punishment before establishing a crime appeared incidental. As the debate raged as to what should happen to Rangers, it was made explicit that our support – the single largest in Scotland – was not to be consulted at any point. When journalists spoke of 'listening to the fans' it was with the caveat, 'not including that lot.'

This was simply the logical extension of the dehumanising process which had been carried out by the media in Scotland on Rangers fans for around a decade. We were not to be thought of as individuals, as people, because that would elicit a far softer reaction. Instead we were 'The Rangers Support' – one collective unit, to be spoken about, labelled, prodded and abused. There was to be no sensible discussion, and if ever one was to be threatened, someone would be sent out to shout 'bigots' and then turn the conversation back to punishments again. The votes were in. The irony in being judged by people who are so hate-filled that they can't even accept any level of debate is almost beyond parody.

But Rangers FC played their part in that. It seemed that Sir David Murray lost interest in Rangers sometime around 2002. He appeared less interested in the football than he was in doing deals, and if this was *raison d'etre* for owning a football club then, when the transfer window was introduced, it massively reduced the time he could spend shopping. Murray's apparent apathy was best exemplified by a media strategy which said 'anything goes.' No matter the slight, no matter the source, he didn't seem to care enough to fix it – the bare minimum was in place. And if those troublesome supporters complained, who cares? He'd signed Gazza and Laudrup after all.

When an empire grows fat and slothful, it usually ends up being dismantled. That was what was happening at Ibrox. Enemies, emboldened by the realisation that Rangers were never going to draw a line in the sand, were now brazenly plotting what they could do to damage the club. The BBC Scotland team seemed almost contemptuous in its dislike. The rest of the media knew they could do what they liked with no reprisals. It's also important to factor into this how utterly divided the Rangers support was. There was no agreement, no consensus, about any of the main issues facing the club. To be brutal, there was not even a desire to accept that there *were* issues facing the club. Many preferred to pretend that debt, the constant downsizing of the playing squad, the inability to sign new players for two years, the shambolic state of the stadium and the impending disaster that was the First Tier Tax Tribunal were insignificant, inventions of malcontents out for their own advancement. Murray had encouraged these divisions for years. A divided support was never going to unite and seriously question the truly abysmal job he was doing.

That said, it's questionable whether there was any real appetite to do so. I acted as the spokesman for the Rangers Supporters Trust (RST) between 2005 and 2010. In that time, we issued many warnings about the parlous state of both the club's finances and the direction it was taking. It's not unfair to say that the vast majority of supporters simply did not want to hear that message. I understood that stance and the reasons for it; we were presenting a picture of a possible financial catastrophe – one which had no easy solutions and one which could take us years to fully recover from. The club was also telling the fans that the Trust and other dissenting voices were just troublemakers, intent on getting attention and trying to cause disharmony amongst the support. From our point of view this was inaccurate but it was gratefully taken as fact by those who wanted it to be true. Hell, even we wanted it to be true. The problem was that, in the end, it wasn't. In 2010, Walter Smith stated publicly for the first time that the club was being run by 'the bank' (Lloyds-HBoS). In the ensuing furore, I mentioned that there was a realistic prospect that we could end up like Leeds United. I recall being inundated with complaints that I was a fantasist and self-publicist intent on creating interest in myself and my organisation with outlandish claims.

I really wish I had been. I wish they were right. I wish I was wrong. But I wasn't. So when the meltdown came, many were abjectly unprepared for it. The Rangers support was divided, slothful, confused and frightened. We were experiencing the worst trauma in forty years at the time we were least equipped to deal with it. So far, so gloomy. However, there was light at the end of this particularly murky tunnel. What happened to us through the nightmare of administration and liquidation is covered elsewhere in the book. However, out of the suffering came a heartening realisation – that if we do the right things going forward, this could well end up being the best thing that ever happened to us. We awoke from our slumber, replaced the fear with vigour and drove onwards. While we have a long way to go, the timid, lazy support of the past may well be assigned to the history books.

The first sign that something was happening came with the march to Hampden on April 28 2012 to protest against the Scottish Football Association's decision to impose a £160,000 fine – against a club in administration – and 12 month registration embargo on the club. What began as an idea on fans forums quickly gathered momentum, with around 10,000 Bears taking to the streets for what was a peaceful protest against the shameless witch-hunt which was by then in full flow. People used to ask why the RST didn't call for protests during the Murray reign. The reason was simple – we didn't think anyone would turn up. It was considered by many in our support to be something the other lot did. For Gers fans to turn out in such numbers – more than attended the matches in the SPL that weekend – told its own story. The fans were waking from their slumber and realising what was happening. More importantly, they were realising that they didn't need to be passive participants in this drama. This was no longer something that was merely happening to them. Protests began to be heard in the stadium about, among other things, possible liquidation, the potential arrival as owner of Bill Miller and the treatment the club were receiving at the hands of the football authorities. Now, it's unlikely that any of these had much effect – you don't get up after a major operation and run a marathon – but these faltering, stumbling steps could prove to be absolutely pivotal in the development of our club.

I'd argue that the passivity of the modern Rangers fan was born out of contentment with what was being served to them. When David Murray was at his zenith, he was an impossibly magnetic figure and he acted as a sugar daddy. The problem with this parental approach was that it allowed the support to infantilise itself. We stopped questioning, accepting our roles as the children in Murray's patriarchy. Sure, we would complain and stamp our feet from time to time, but it was accepted that the decisions were to be taken by the grown-up. This suited most parties while Murray could keep us entertained with signings and trophies. When he couldn't, the support engaged in a mass delusion that nothing had changed or, if it had, it was temporary. When the new reality brought everyone kicking and screaming towards the actualities of the situation, Rangers fans were shorn of their comfort blankets. We were cold, we were angry – but we were motivated.

Charles Green has spoken of how fans wanted to lynch him on his arrival in Glasgow. He was right and he was wrong simultaneously. The fans were *desperate* to get behind someone. They had mobilised and they wanted a flag, a banner to rally to. But after what had happened to us, how could we be expected to trust anyone? Amid a morass of conflicting information, Green was just another stranger telling us things which may or may not – and still may or may not – be true. Walter Smith and Jim McColl's attempted takeover after liquidation was, for many, the breaking point. When it failed, it seemed that even the most reliable of Rangers men couldn't help us. The fact was that while many were willing to tell us why other people were wrong, they couldn't deliver when the time came for them to step up. Fans decided to reluctantly pitch in behind Green.

And this is where the positive changes started to take effect. Green is a clever man and he realised immediately something that no-one else had seemed to grasp – Rangers fans want to give Rangers money. They will do so, happily, if you are nice to them. Green began a studious and ultimately successful attempt to woo us. He spoke at supporters functions, he talked to fans outside the stadium. He made resolutely populist noises about the SFA, the SPL and its member clubs and the press. He played to the gallery, a fact that seemed to annoy the many detractors of the club. But it was entirely sound business strategy. Yes he was pandering to the fans, as the press indicated, but he was also pandering to his customers. And only within Scottish football, and only then to one club within it, would that be cause for criticism. Curiously, it's seen as an insult to say a club owner 'only wants the fans money.' I actually have far more confidence in someone like that than some megalomaniac who is doing it to fuel his ego. If someone does things the way I want, I'm happy to give my money to them. It's the very definition of a win/win scenario.

Nowhere is this more prevalent than in communication. We live in a post-internet world. The traditional models of information delivery have been decimated. Print, radio and TV – while still reasonably useful – are no longer the standard modes of getting your message out. With web and club channels, as well as social media, there is now huge opportunity for the club and the support to bypass journalists and communicate directly. Should the club wish to get information out to their supporters, then they can do so without having to filter it through the prism of press attention. The other side of that coin is fans directly communicating with the club. While this removes a barrier – and make no mistake, the Fourth Estate in Scotland is a significant barrier for Rangers – it means there can be none of the dismissive, put-upon, everything-is-too-much-trouble attitude which held sway at Ibrox for the last decade. Fans want to be courted. Fans want to be listened to.

Rangers' presence across web and social media platforms such as Twitter and Facebook improved exponentially in 2012. By constantly looking for ways to engage the support, they have opened up a clear and direct route for supporters to interact with the club without having to go through a conduit such as Radio Clyde. This has built a feeling of inclusiveness and, more importantly, significantly reduced the chasm between those employed by the club and those who follow it. The feeling that we are all in this together is a valuable asset for Rangers. Fans will have far more tolerance and understanding of mistakes they feel were made by genuine people with the same passion for the club that they have. To see players on Twitter talking about the match day experience, the city, other big matches going on – anything – humanises them and draws them closer to the people who pay to see them. This is almost lost at a club of our size – it was certainly dead up until this season – but it makes every supporter's heart beat a little faster to think that we are all pushing for the same thing together. At most big clubs in modern football it often appears that the fans are there for love, and the staff are there for money. Not so at Ibrox these days. Is it an illusion? Who cares! So long as the perception is that of unity, it feeds on itself in a wholly virtuous cycle.

Speaking of perception, it is now apparent that Rangers supporters believe that the media in Scotland has an agenda against them and their club. When faced with criticism on this subject, the BBC, Radio Clyde and their ilk tend to haughtily dismiss these claims as paranoia. This is an insidious form of defence, because when anyone accused of paranoia speaks up to defend themselves of the charge, everything they say is invariably used as more evidence of their guilt. It's risible. I could list dozens of examples of shameful treatment handed down to both Rangers and us as fans by so-called neutral outlets, but really, why bother? I recall a well-kent voice from the BBC telling me that the BBC Scotland office is 'riddled' with people who absolutely despise Rangers, not merely due to football loyalties, but due to a misplaced belief in the singularity of politics among our support. They have created an image of us as right-wing, pro-Union, Orange walking clichés. The idea that there is a massive plurality among our support is anathema to them, so locked are they in their own simplistic view of the world, with shop-bought ideology straight out of a 1982 copy of their University newspaper. Let's stop participating in the charade. They know what their agenda is; we can clearly see what their agenda is, let us be grown-ups and move on even if they can't.

Rangers fans now increasingly get their news from the club and from their fellow fans. The rise in stature of blogs such as *The Rangers Standard* means Rangers fans can get sensible, adult analysis of the club and its place in society from people who feel the same way they do. They can then discuss them on Rangers-only message boards across the various forums. You could argue that such segregation is perhaps sad, but the rest of Scottish football isn't interested in discussing issues with us like sensible humans. The Rangers Family is turning inward towards self-sufficiency. It is a model which can only do us good. Rangers' online TV station is in its infancy, but live coverage of matches this season on a pay-per-view basis has been excellent, and preferable to watching on television. Any Rangers fan listening to the BBC or Radio Clyde, by now, deserves all they get. Let's leave them to it, even if they seem incapable of doing the same to us. It's just jealousy stemming from a well-deserved inferiority complex. If Rangers fans can spend the money that they currently spend on newspapers and media on the club, rather than third party providers, then it would seem that no-one except the old media loses.

The crowd at Ibrox is changing. It has been noticeable this season that the demographic make-up has changed. Encouraged by cheaper prices, more families have started going, bringing with them a new vitality and reminding some of the more jaded among us of the joy in watching your team. To be fair, most of us had rediscovered that early on in 2012 – the thought of not having a club to follow made us appreciate the simple act of doing so a hell of a lot more. Previously, surly fans would turn up with what I jokingly called the 'Nirvana' attitude of 'here we are now, entertain us.' While not saying we have quite achieved a state of mental bliss watching our performances – some of which, in the

2012–13 season, have been inept – we've maybe started to realise that there's more to this than whether their winger keeps going past our full-back. We are developing a new generation of fans, something not happening at other clubs where cost is limiting family attendance and kids are growing up without getting into the habit of match day being a huge part of their week. That simply won't happen with us, and we'll reap the benefits of it a decade hence. These guys will be the lifeblood of the club over the coming years.

This, for me, is the biggest change. While some still cling to the idea that every single match is a matter of life and death, it really isn't. 2012 helped us gain a bit of perspective into what really matters to us as supporters. Rangers have been a cornerstone of my identity since I was a child; the idea of it not existing any more scared me immensely. Indeed, my love for the club is probably deeper than is intellectually sensible, but it doesn't matter. I love the old place so dearly that life without it is simply unimaginable. When I was faced with a glimpse of that possible future, like every other Gers supporter, it terrified me to my very core. I'm never going to take Rangers for granted again.

Moving forward, Rangers need to introduce a new management structure which is similar to the European model, namely the coach coaches the players and the official runs the club. The rule that a manager selects every single signing is considered sacrosanct in the UK, but it is a silly and outmoded idea. Managers come and go based on results – the club needs to be stable regardless. A boss should always be hired on the basis of his ability to get the best from the playing squad, not to demand a huge transfer kitty and bring in better players. We've tried that. It doesn't work. We need to focus on youth development, at all levels. Young players have been receiving far more game time since summer 2012 and this must continue. Some of them will, inevitably, not make it. We must accept failure will be a necessary evil in achieving success. Our scouting has to improve. There can be no blame attached to anyone at the club for the signings made before the 2012–13 season as chaos raged around us, but signing players who we've all heard of from Scotland is not the way to go. Have a core of experienced players then surround them with the most promising youngsters in the country. Make sure we have academies set up in far-flung corners of the globe so we are well-placed to develop international talent. Then accept – and this will be hard for some fans – that we will need to sell the best of these to keep the club running sensibly. Do not buy players we don't need and give them long contracts. Have a wage cap at the club, and stick to it.

Managers in the UK seem to recoil in horror when asked to justify sign-ings but that can't happen at Rangers. If the manager wants a player, we need to know why. If you have two full-backs and a youngster in the reserves, you're not getting another. If you really want him, get rid of one of the others first. Every pound must be accounted for and justified.

That will sound like heresy to some of our support, but it needs to be implemented and then followed with ruthless efficiency. I never, ever, want the very future of our club gambled with in the quest for short-term success. Do this sensibly and, with our support behind us, we'll always be in contention when it comes to prize-giving time. Our fanatical sup-port provides us with an incredible advantage over most of our rivals.

Rangers are back from the brink, and as we come up, we'll be looking to exact some revenge on the football pitch. It's as simple as that. The fans will not soon forget those who treated us poorly in our hour of need. They've woken a tiger, and it is one which is focused and hungry. Rangers supporters proved in 2012 that the only place we're going is to watch our team in massive numbers. We will never again allow ourselves to be in the position we were in. There has to be a realignment of our expectations, aims and goals. All we ask is that those in charge make Rangers the best we can possibly be and remember that we will be watching them. I believe that all our travails will make us stronger, and that history will record that this was the time when a new generation of fans discovered, and others rediscovered, what it is to be a Rangers Supporter. That this club means the world and more to us has never been in doubt, but famil-iarity had indeed bred contempt. Never again.

And for everyone else? We are coming. Expect us.

CHAPTER XIII

Time for Followers to become Leaders

RICHARD WILSON

WHAT HAPPENED TO RANGERS? Asked at different stages of the saga that befell the club, the question would generate different answers. Yet in essence what occurred was that the supporters had to reconsider what the club meant to them. When Rangers needed saved, and when the fans were able to intervene, they acted in a selfless way that so many others involved in the club's fate were incapable of. Individuals cluttered around the scene claiming credit, and there is still a narrative that tries to establish Charles Green as the figure who rescued the club, but that is to misunderstand what happened. It must also be said, though, that the supporters were also guilty of misreading the situation. This was not just a moment of crisis, it was also an opportunity.

Of all the attempts to understand what happened to Rangers, the most revealing is to look at what happened to the fans; or specifically, their relationship to the club. Under Sir David Murray, the Rangers support became disenfranchised. It was a slow process, this passivity, not least because most of the years under his ownership were hugely successful. Fans became sated by the constant renewal of triumph, but Murray changed the very nature of the club, its psyche. Rangers became brash, arrogant even, and began to take glory for granted, as well as presenting a kind of conceited disdain for others.

This was in contrast to many of the values that previous generations had cherished, but there was no disquiet when trophies and ambitions were always being accumulated. When the financial reality of Murray's time began to unravel, what was most striking was the schism that had developed between the club and its fans. They bought season tickets in vast numbers, they turned up for games in vast numbers, they bought merchandise in vast numbers, but they were not active, they were not engaged, with the politics or the business of the club. Murray had not encouraged that kind of relationship between the fans and their team, while the majority of supporters had not seen the need to pursue it.

As the sole steward during the time that football finances across the world grew disproportionately massive, turning the game into a lucrative business — mostly through broadcast contracts — a mindset was established under Murray. That of the benefactor owner: the rich individual with the particular nous and the resources to maintain the club's success. The fans were, essentially, disengaged. They were not needed, in this scenario, other than as powerless background characters in a play. Dissenting voices eventually began to grow, and Murray soon had fierce critics among the fan base, but they were marginal among the sheer size of the club's following as a whole; there was no vast movement, of ideas or rhetoric, or campaigning. By the time the full extent of the big tax case became known, as well as Murray's failure to find a buyer, there was not the means amongst the support to collectively respond.

That is not to dismiss the efforts of the Rangers Supporters Trust and all who have served that organisation down the years. They worked hard against the prevailing mood. Under Murray, as different fan groups were organised, the support became splintered. What Craig Whyte and then Green were able to do was briefly unite the majority, by playing to their sense of injustice over particular matters. Whyte railed against the media, and Green railed against the football authorities. For a time, that was enough to secure them some crucial backing, and the fans were simply responding to their disenfranchisement, since they enthusiastically welcomed a figure — who was essentially unknown — because he was prepared to stand up for them, to voice support for them, in a way that the previous regime had not. There was an over-reliance on the cult of the personality. Yet this is the crux of the matter: it was the fans, in buying season tickets, merchandise and the other means by which they part with their money for the club, who sustained Rangers.

This is the same for all teams, no matter their size or ambition. Manchester United, Barcelona and Bayern Munich can rely on huge commercial revenue streams, but only because they are big, successful clubs. They all count upon the size of their support, in their stadiums but also in their broadcast and sponsorship deals, since those too reach out to the extended fan base. Other clubs that have tried to compete on this scale, such as Chelsea, or Manchester City, or Paris St Germain, can only do so through the benefactor model. They sought accelerated growth, but their ambition and success is underwritten by the enormous wealth of their owners, and even the triumphs that are celebrated cannot buy the prestige, history, heritage and supporter constituency of the likes of United and Barcelona. Take away the benefactors, and the clubs cannot compete.

Rangers, in a sense, came to straddle both definitions. When they were owned by Murray, the effect was to present the notion of a benefactor model, yet he was never truly underwriting the club's business. Rangers also possess the stature, the traditions, the long-established foundations. Murray's tenure, which brought nine-in-a-row, as well as the sophisticated, and brief, brilliance of Dick Advocaat's team, also undermined Rangers. Once Whyte's charade was fully revealed, through the non-payment of PAYE and VAT, and administration put the club on the market again, there was no coherent fan movement to step up.

Instead, supporters argued amongst themselves about the merits of the various different interested parties. Some backed the Blue Knights, others wanted a clean break from the past so were more inclined towards Bill Ng or Bill Miller. As the administration period dragged on, and the conduct of Duff & Phelps was increasingly criticised by the Knights, Brian Kennedy and others, a particular refrain was often delivered online and publicly: if they're real Rangers men, why don't they put their hands deeper into their pockets? When Green suddenly appeared on the scene, so abruptly and with such an unclear background that it immediately prompted suspicion, the refrain became: where's Jim McColl? Where's Sir Tom Hunter? In effect, where is our rescuer?

This was a direct consequence of the Murray years, the reliance on, or the need for, a redeemer, a sole, wealthy saviour. The RST were working with the Knights to try to deliver a fan ownership model but when the latter's bid stalled, there was not enough momentum for the ordinary supporters themselves to mobilise. Even when Green launched an initial public offering of shares in December 2012, the take-up amongst fans was modest. They were split between buying shares as individuals and buying as part of the RST's initiative, so that the Trust had to subsequently try to establish a proxy scheme so that the roughly 11 per cent shareholding that they all held could be a powerful influence.

There were mitigating circumstances throughout. No buyer was prepared to purchase Rangers from Murray without him agreeing to retain the potential liability of the Big Tax Case, which either Murray or Lloyds Bank were not prepared to accept. There were lingering suspicions of Green and his consortium ahead of the IPO, although raising significant amounts from institutional investors also removed much of the urgency for supporters to dig deep. Even still, the story of Rangers, the fall and the rise, has involved the re-engagement of the fans without a coherent strategy for making the most important move of all: purchasing a controlling stake themselves. It is now a long-term aim, with the RST hoping that their BuyRangers scheme will eventually hold a large stake in the club, but even as Green's regime unravelled in the summer of 2013, only 12 months on from the consortium he fronted purchasing the club, the wait again was for a new saviour: a Dave King, McColl again, perhaps Ng. Anybody, that is, apart from the fans themselves.

The story of Rangers had become a financial one, of administration, company liquidation, tax bills, assets, revenue streams, debts, company voluntary arrangements, share purchase agreements, but also of social, political, cultural and media influences; and at times, the lack of them. As the club's finances collapsed, the reactions — inside and outside the game — were telling. It brought us to the very heart of understanding what a football club is, which is the emotional commitment and loyalty of its supporters. As an institution, Rangers remains best understood by its history of success, the glories and the triumphs of the past, of its founding story and the way it established itself as Scotland's leading club, but the rise again from administration and then the liquidation of Rangers Football Club PLC is a clearer representation of what football itself means.

It is an expression of identity, of cultural importance, but also a form of belonging; it has a social benefit. Sport is, of course, little more than a distraction from the demands and the realities of life, but it is too embedded in our society to be dismissed as a frivolity. Many Rangers supporters spent money on season tickets that they might have more prudently spent on other essentials. Why? Because their club matters to them. They filled Ibrox throughout administration and then the campaign in the Third Division. Why? Because they are committed to their club. Glasgow reverberates to the cheers and sighs of the game; mention to somebody in the city that you don't like football, or don't follow a particular team of your own, and they will look at you askance. Few places in the world possess such a deep connection with the game that it reaches into every part of life, the personal, the cultural, the social, the political and the religious.

Rangers owners throughout history have both valued and taken advantage of the loyalty of the fans. It is the strongest foundation of the club and yet not always capable of sustaining it alone because Rangers have never been opened to the notion of supporter ownership, in any form, at least until the summer of 2012. Murray racked up debts then embarked on a tax scheme that was so risky that the prospect alone of the potential bill ultimately delivered the club into the hands of an unscrupulous owner. Whyte's short, catastrophic regime then led to another group of owners whose intention was to make as much money as they could from the club. Many fans understood this to mean that their team would be revived because that would deliver the best return for the investors. Yet in football there will always come a breaking point between the profit motive and the sporting one.

Green's regime never encountered that — it usually comes in the balance between dividends to shareholders and investment in the team — because it fell apart so quickly. Even the supporters who could see that he was a salesman, and an expressive and remarkably effective one at that, allowed themselves to be swayed, as did investors. The IPO was a huge success, because Green sold a vision, and because it was clear that the value of the club would grow as it climbed the divisions. Rangers were to be run as a business, corporately lean and focused on new markets and revenue streams, but it turned out that Green and Imran Ahmad, the real power behind the consortium, did not possess the means to deliver on their business plan or aims. Green was not a conventional chief executive and Ahmad was trying to drive the business from the back seat; they could not adapt to their surroundings. As progress was lost to egotism, the manager Ally McCoist became wary, then the chairman, Malcolm Murray, sensed an opportunity to oust the regime. Green and Ahmad may have eventually hit the wall anyway, since their expertise is in investment and the stock market, not running a football club, particularly one with such a high profile and influential reach as Rangers. Either way, in the summer following the administration of 2012, Rangers fans were again being asked to buy season tickets to ensure the ongoing revival of their club.

This recurring theme cannot be ignored. Some potential bidders for the club talked privately about trying to drive down the share price once Green and Ahmad had left the club in May 2013 because they wanted to maximise how much they could invest once they had bought it. At the same time, they were expecting the fragile financial position within the club to cause the share price to fall. It was a precarious balance. This fits in with the culture of spending incoming money to bring success, and in football the clubs that have the highest wage bills tend to enjoy a competitive advantage. Nonetheless, the relationship between Rangers and its supporters still needs to be addressed, particularly if the club is to thrive for another 140 years. What kind of club do the fans want? Now, along with wanting a successful one, they might wish for an institution that they can influence, that they can be an active part of.

The business of football is dysfunctional. Clubs can turn over millions of pounds, figures that are grossly disproportionate to the actual size of the institutions themselves. Media money, particularly from television, has distorted the old values, of prudence and patience. The Rangers support became accustomed to this way of operating, as Murray brought new signings to Glasgow in his private jet, often with Sir Sean Connery in tow. This expensive, elitist attitude is often confused with the widespread sense of Rangers being the establishment club. Yet this older identity is one that gathers together values such as dignity, pride, industry, of a certain ethical propriety. Those core values were crushed during football's boom years, partly by the flood of money that was readily available.

The relationship between fans and their club was once simple: when they turned up to watch matches at their home ground, they were funding their team. This became more complex as merchandising and other forms of commercialisation grew, then television deals seemed to belittle the importance of match attendance. At the same time, football became a capitalist venture, a form of raising and making profits. For a time, this seemed to be a kind of nirvana, but then media partners failed, administrations loomed and only a small elite — the Champions League clubs — could continue to grow at an inordinate rate.

Rangers were part of this time, in their own way. Yet football isn't a business, not in the strict sense. Clubs exist not to make profit, but to sustain hopes and dreams, to be a form of sustenance, emotionally and socially. Profit means nothing to supporters. Clubs ought to be run, at all levels, as not-for-profit, mutually-owned organisations. Supporters Direct and the Government have championed such schemes, and there is enough advice and support out there for the only excuse to be a lack of commitment to the idea itself. What can proper fan engagement achieve? Look at Borussia Dortmund, a club that suffered its own financial catastrophe, but fought back from the brink through a three-way relationship. The club, its supporters, and the local community in Dortmund – both socially and politically – worked together to restore Borussia. The stadium now regularly fills its 80,000 capacity, and the team competed in the 2013 Champions League final, losing to Bayern Munich.

There are alternatives, and Community Interest Companies can be set up, run with funds from investors, but not for profit, and with the assets held in trust so that they cannot be sold off or mortgaged. This mirrors the plc, in that investors can provide funds in return for dividends, but with all management decisions made for the benefit of the community — in this case the club's supporters and the Scottish game itself. Clubs exist in and because of their local (or in some cases, national or international) community. They are part of the fabric of a city, a town, a suburb, even a country and a diaspora, and so they ought to protect themselves from the potential pitfalls of capitalism. Raising money through revenue is necessary, but it should all be held within the club, spent on the fundamentals like the first-team, the youth set-up, coaching, medicine, scouting.

British football has been wary, and at times downright distrustful, of supporter-ownership models. These are part of the very notion of the game in other countries in Europe, but starting them from scratch in the UK allows all the doubts and quirks of the idea to be amplified. In short, though, they are a form of protection. If fans, collectively, own 51 per cent of their clubs, then ruinous ownership can be avoided because there is an element of control. Executive management teams can be appointed and allowed to run the business as they would be if the club was owned by a publicly limited company. The beauty of the scheme devised by Green and Ahmad was that with so many small shareholders – Green was the highest individual shareholder when he left the club with a 7.8 per cent stake — they did not need to wait for one person or company to come along and make a bid for ownership. Their shares could be picked off by other investors over a short period of time, allowing them to realise their personal profit quickly.

Being launched on the Alternative Investment Market offered a form of protection for Rangers, because the company that owned the club, Rangers International Football Club, had to be bought, sold and owned within the confines of the AIM rules. Yet there was no ultimate backstop against more ruthless owners taking control again. Green and Ahmad, after all, made their move in the summer of 2012 because they saw that for £5.5m they could buy the business and assets of Rangers Football Club PLC, which were worth several times more, even on a bad day. The support, however, could not move so swiftly to raise that kind of money.

There was an issue, too, with the professional classes. The lawyers, bankers, accountants and the like who were Rangers supporters but had also been disenfranchised under Murray, who ran the club his own way. They were not engaged, either with the club or with each other, in a way that was needed during the chaotic weeks and months that followed administration. The expertise, contacts and knowledge that the fan base needed just to understand the club's predicament, let alone act on it, was not available out with small, individual groups. Progress might have been made had there been figures to rally around within the fan base, but factionalism was too prevalent.

There is still, though, an opportunity to redress the balance. Green talked about enabling fan ownership, but that was rhetoric. It can only be small progress towards that goal, but participation and engagement are vital. One of the plans that the Green regime was working towards was a membership scheme, which is one way to draw the wider supporter base out of established cliques, but there needs to be more than simply paying scant notice to what it means to re-engage the fans. Football's traditionalists balk at the idea of fans sitting on the board, but most clubs have a wide enough background of supporters that individuals with the requisite knowledge and experience can be elected. The point is engagement, though. Supporting your club needs to be about more than attendance at matches and buying the occasional replica jersey. Fans need to be involved in aspects of the decision making process, they need to be empowered, whether it is voting on certain retained issues — such as kit design or ticket prices or dividends or the wage to turnover ratio — or on selecting the executive management team. For the good of the club itself, for the good of the fans, even for the good of the game, football needs to refresh its relationship with its followers.

Rangers are a prime example of what can happen when a club's owners lose sight of their limitations, or when a club is bought over by individuals who only have their own interests at heart. It used to be that those who ran a football team were described as custodians. This can seem a little antiquated now, but it is exactly true. They look after the club for a moment of time in its history. The prime motivation is to be successful, but also to ensure that it remains strong, healthy and vibrant for the next generation.

Rangers supporters endured pain and trauma as administration then liquidation swallowed up Rangers Football Club PLC, and during the events that followed. Their support, the very meaning of their relationship with the club, was stripped down to bare essentials. They had to respond, and they did, but so much more could have been achieved. Those who run Rangers in the future must learn lessons from this period, but so too must the support. The club would have died without them, but they are also better placed than anybody else to prevent that from happening again.

They need to mobilise, they need to take control of their club, even if it takes years to achieve, and they need to become actively engaged in how the business is operated. It is their club; they, too, pass it on to the next generation.

Luath Press Limited
committed to publishing well written books worth reading

LUATH PRESS takes its name from Robert Burns, whose little collie Luath (*Gael.,* swift or nimble) tripped up Jean Armour at a wedding and gave him the chance to speak to the woman who was to be his wife and the abiding love of his life. Burns called one of 'The Twa Dogs' Luath after Cuchullin's hunting dog in Ossian's *Fingal*. Luath Press was established in 1981 in the heart of Burns country, and is now based a few steps up the road from Burns' first lodgings on Edinburgh's Royal Mile.
Luath offers you distinctive writing with a hint of unexpected pleasures.

Most bookshops in the UK, the US, Canada, Australia, New Zealand and parts of Europe either carry our books in stock or can order them for you. To order direct from us, please send a £sterling cheque, postal order, international money order or your credit card details (number, address of cardholder and expiry date) to us at the address below. Please add post and packing as follows: UK – £1.00 per delivery address; overseas surface mail – £2.50 per delivery address; overseas air-mail – £3.50 for the first book to each delivery address, plus £1.00 for each additional book by airmail to the same address. If your order is a gift, we will happily enclose your card or message at no extra charge.

ILLUSTRATION: IAN KELLAS

Luath Press Limited
543/2 Castlehill
The Royal Mile
Edinburgh EH1 2ND
Scotland
Telephone: 0131 225 4326 (24 hours)
Fax: 0131 225 4324
email: sales@luath.co.uk
Website: www.luath.co.uk

Stramash: Tackling Scotland's Towns and Teams

Daniel Gray
ISBN 978 1906817 66 4 PBK £9.99

Fatigued by bloated big-time football and bored of samey big cities, Daniel Gray went in search of small town Scotland and its teams. Part travelogue, part history, and part mistakenly spilling ketchup on the face of a small child, *Stramash* takes an uplifting look at the counties nether regions.

Using the excuse of a match to visit places from Dumfries to Dingwall, *Stramash* accomplishes the feats of visiting Dumfries without mentioning Robert Burns, being positive about Cumbernauld and linking Elgin City to Lenin. It is ae fond look at Scotland as you've never seen it before.

There have been previous attempts by authors to explore the off-the-beaten paths of the Scottish football landscape, but Daniel Gray's volume is in another league.
THE SCOTSMAN

A brilliant way to rediscover Scotland.
THE HERALD

100 Favourite Scottish Football Poems

Edited by Alistair Findlay
ISBN 978 1906307 03 5 PBK £7.99

Poems to evoke the roar of the crowd. Poems to evoke the collective groans. Poems to capture the elation. Poems to capture the heartbreak. Poems by fans. Poems by critics. Poems about the highs and lows of Scottish football.

This collection captures the passion Scots feel about football, covering every aspect of the game, from World Cup heartbreak to one-on-ones with the goalie. Feel the thump of the tackle, the thrill of victory and the expectation of supporters. Become immersed in the emotion and personality of the game as these poems reflect human experience in its sheer diversity of feeling and being. The collection brings together popular culture with literature, fan with critic, and brings together subject matters as unlikely as the header and philosophy.

[this book] *brings home the dramatic and emotional potential that's latent in the beautiful game.*
THE LIST

Is the Baw Burst?

Iain Hyslop

Volume 1:
ISBN 978 1 908373 22 9 PBK £9.99

Volume 2:
ISBN 978 1 908373 55 7 PBK £9.99

Volume 3:
ISBN 978 1 908373 78 6 PBK £9.99

Football has to wake up to reality and get its house in order. Brave decisions must be taken and followed through. Huge changes are needed.
Financial problems, falling attendances, poor quality football, crumbling stadiums, terrible catering… is the picture really as bad as it's painted? Time to have a look.
IAIN HYSLOP

In season 2010/11, Iain Hyslop embarked on a journey which would take him to 44 football matches, from Peterhead to Berwick and Dingwall to Dumfries, across a single season. His travels led to the first volume of *Is the Baw Burst?*; an unofficial review of Scottish football.

But then disaster struck for the die-hard Rangers fan. He decided to continue his search for the soul of Scottish football by following his team through their season in the Third Division. Volumes 2 and 3 of *Is the Baw Burst?*, which include interviews with fans from all walks of life, are the result of this remarkable season.

Asking how the recent turmoil will affect the beautiful game in Scotland, Hyslop represents the voices in the bar-room boardrooms across the country. But ultimately he is searching for the answer to the question on everyone's lips: Is the Baw Burst?

This view from the not-so-cheap seats (Hyslop is adamant that football has to be more realistic with its pricing policy) ought to be required reading for everyone involved at the top end of the game.
THE SCOTSMAN

Singin I'm No a Billy He's a Tim

Des Dillon
ISBN 978 1 908373 05 2 PBK £6.99

What happens when you lock up a Celtic fan?

What happens when you lock up a Celtic fan with a Rangers fan?

What happens when you lock up a Celtic fan with a Rangers fan on the day of the Old Firm match?

Des Dillon watches the sparks fly as Billy and Tim clash in a rage of sectarianism and deep-seated hatred. When children have been steeped in bigotry since birth, is it possible for them to change their views?

Join Billy and Tim on their journey of discovery. Are you singing their tune?

Explosive.
EVENING NEWS

His raucous sense of humour and keen understanding of the west-coast sectarian mindset make his sisters-under-the-skin message seem a matter of urgency and not just a liberal platitude.
THE GUARDIAN

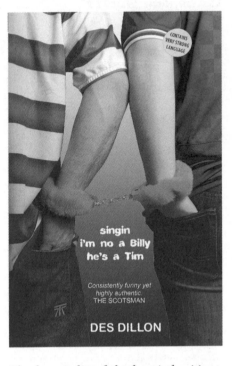

The sheer vitality of the theatrical writing – the seamless combination of verbal wit and raw kinetic energy, and the pure dynamic strength of the play's structure – makes [Singin I'm No a Billy He's a Tim] *feel like one of the shortest and most gripping two-hour shows in current Scottish theatre.*
THE SCOTSMAN